TABLE OF CONTENTS

i

ABOUT THE AUTHOR

John J. Tierney, Jr., is an Adjunct Associate Professor of Political Science at the Catholic University of America. He has also taught at the University of Virginia and at Johns Hopkins University. A former Public Affairs Fellow at the Hoover Institution at Stanford, California, he has been a consultant to the Heritage Foundation in Washington, D.C. Dr. Tierney is currently an official with the U.S. Arms Control and Disarmament Agency. He received his Ph.D. from the University of Pennsylvania, where he wrote his dissertation on Augusto Sandino and the Marine Corps intervention in Nicaragua.

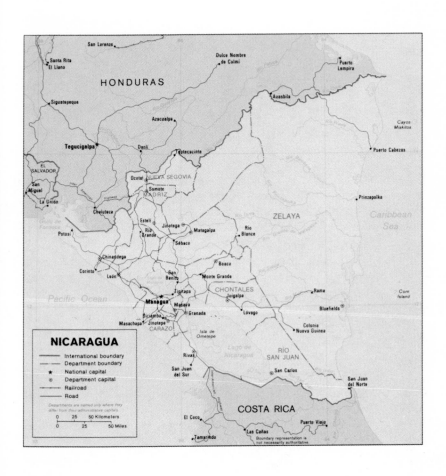

HONDURAS

San Lorenzo

Saota Rita
El Llano

Siguatepeque

Tegucigalpa ★

Danli

Azacualpa

Dulce Nombre
de Culmi

Auasbila

Puerto
Lempira

Cayos
Miskitos

Puerto Cabezas

Totocacinte

EL
SALVADOR

San
Miguel

La Unión

Cheluteca

Ocotal NUEVA SEGOVIA

Somoto
MADRIZ

Prinzapolka

ZELAYA

Caribbean
Sea

Potosi

Esteli

Jinotega

Río
Grande

Matagalpa

Río
Blanco

Sebaco

Chinandega

Corinto

León

San
Benito

Boaca

Monte Grande

CHONTALES
Juigalpa

Rama

Corn
Island

Pacific Ocean

Managua ★

Matava

Tipitapa

Bluefields

Diriamba

Masachapa

Jinotepe

CARAZO

Granada

Isla de
Ometepe

Lóvago

Colonia
Nueva Guinea

Lago de
Nicaragua

RÍO
SAN JUAN

Rivas

San Juan
del Sur

San Carlos

San Juan
del Norte

COSTA RICA

El Coco

Puerto Viejo

Tamarindo

Las Cañas

Boundary representation is
not necessarily authoritative.

NICARAGUA

—— International boundary
---- Department boundary
★   National capital
⊛   Department capital
+++ Railroad
—— Road

Departments are named only where they
differ from their administrative capitals.

0   25   50 Kilometers
0   25   50 Miles

PREFACE

In September 1980, the exiled former President of Nicaragua Anastasio Somoza Debayle ("Tacho") was shot to death on the streets of Asunción, Paraguay. Somoza's violent demise came in the same manner as that of his father before him, who was killed by an assassin in 1956. Both father and son had presided over the government of Nicaragua which, including another son, Luis, spanned a dynasty of 43 years. The Somoza dynasty itself was created by violence, including a long civil war between Nicaragua's two political parties, plus nearly six years of guerrilla conflict between independent Sandinistas and U.S. Marines.

The death of Somoza III has not ended the characteristic conflicts of Nicaraguan politics. They continue today, but in a totalitarian political system unknown to the *caudillos* of the Somozas' Nicaragua or the old dictators who ruled before them.

The stormy history of Nicaragua and the U.S. in the twentieth century is still unfolding today. Few Americans are probably aware of the continuity between the Somozas and the Sandinistas in this century. The end of the first Sandinistas in 1934 helped create the first Somoza government in 1936. The end of the last Somoza regime in 1979 created the first Sandinista government.

Today, that government is at odds with the United States, a sizeable portion of its own citizenry plus several neighboring governments in Central America. Nicaragua has charted a determined course toward alignment with the U.S.S.R. and Cuba. It is also actively supporting revolution in El Salvador, and has joined the radical segment of "third world" ideologue states. This has put Nicaragua on a direct collision course with the United States.

After many years of unconcern, the issue of Nicaragua has once again become a live and controversial one in world politics. The harsh anti-U.S. rhetoric of the Sandinistas has begun to reach the American public, and this rhetoric has on occasion been matched by equally

v

sharp comments from U.S. officials. There is talk of intervention, blockade, paramilitary forces, etc. The United Nations has taken up the case, and the problems between the U.S. and Nicaragua have again become headline news in the American media. Guerrilla and terrorist violence in neighboring El Salvador and Guatemala has served only to heighten U.S. interest in Nicaragua. Nevertheless, there is a long background to this, a story of which very few Americans are probably aware.

The following chapters concisely relate the most important points in this long historic compass. This book is an attempt to summarize history, with the hope that the present generation will be provided the necessary perspective on a current topic which promises, true to the past, more controversy and danger—with the strong possibility of even more violence than before.

My thesis, quite simply, is that one can see much more through a "telescope" than a "microscope." By examining the spectrum of the history of the United States and Nicaragua during this century, one sees a clearer picture of the momentum of events upon current affairs. Background is an essential part of the present, and the background between the U.S. and Nicaragua is rich in detail and controversy. I have deliberately sacrificed trivial and less-important details in favor of a larger perspective. I do not believe that this is much of a sacrifice.

I have also deliberately omitted obtrusive footnoting, except in direct quotations from public sources. I have tried to keep this book as much of an essay as possible. Private papers which are quoted throughout, especially in Chapters II, III, and IV, are all derived from my own Ph.D. Dissertation (University of Pennsylvania, 1969) on Augusto Sandino and the Marines. Direct references to most of these can be seen in an earlier article, "U.S. Intervention in Nicaragua, 1927-33: Lessons for Today," Orbis, Winter 1971. The bibliography will suffice to demonstrate the range of my own research.

My appreciation goes to my wife, Beatrice, who was especially patient during the long evenings I spent at my desk. My appreciation also goes to Mssrs. Roger Reed and L. Francis Bouchey of the Council for Inter-American Security Educational Institute for the opportunity to publish this narrative. Nobody but myself, however, should take responsibility for the opinions expressed, nor for the style and framework in which they are here presented.

April 7, 1982

I. INTRODUCTION: HISTORY, POLITICS AND STRATEGY

On July 19, 1979, the 43-year rule of the Somoza family in Nicaragua came to an abrupt and violent end. A civil war which killed over 40,000 people replaced President Anastasio Somoza Debayle with a revolutionary coalition led by the victorious Sandinista guerrilla army.

This revolution may be a watershed in Central American history. The Soviet Union and Cuba have already begun turning Nicaragua into a militarized beachhead in Central America. Guerrilla wars in El Salvador and Guatemala have been greatly expanded. Nicaragua's relations with Washington are still in a state of uncertain transition. The outcome of this period of transition will have lasting effects upon the future of the entire region. Not since Fidel Castro's victory in Cuba in 1959 has a Latin American revolution had such an impact—with an equal potential for violence and unrest—upon the countries of the Caribbean and Central America.

Nicaragua is the new Cuba, the first established Marxist-dominated and anti-U.S. regime in the history of Central America.[1] How could this occur, especially within the geopolitical domain of the United States? The answer to this question is far from easy. It involves a deep and complex set of historical issues which transcend both the Carter Administration, which was in power when Somoza fell, and the Somoza family itself, which had governed the country for such a long period of time.

The issue is larger than the personalities and politics of any two administrations. It involves political culture, ideology, and national interest, permanent issues which have determined relations between Washington and Managua throughout the twentieth century. The Sandinista victory may have changed the current definition of those issues, but it cannot—and will not—change their lasting importance.

Nicaragua and the United States are determined by history and geography to share a common interest in the future of Latin America.

1

The present rupture between the two countries, from this perspective, has profound implications. To understand the present, we must telescope the past. Reasons for the current problems have a natural history. The Sandinista revolution did not just happen overnight, and Somoza's problems in keeping his own hold on power were not the single product of an international conspiracy.

To be sure, the Carter Administration played an important role in President Somoza's downfall, just as Cuban and other sources did by assisting the rebels, particularly in the last year of the civil war. But the deeper and more lasting causes of the Sandinista movement go back decades before 1979. To understand both the Somozas and the Sandinistas, we must first appreciate the larger dimensions of U.S.-Nicaraguan relations in the twentieth century. These form a critical backdrop to the present dilemmas.

Nicaraguan Politics

It has never been easy for Americans to fully appreciate the Nicaraguan political system. This was no less true in the Administration of Jimmy Carter than it was of many past U.S. administrations, whether Republican or Democrat. Not only are the two nations completely different in geographic location, economic strength and social composition, but the profound and underlying differences in political culture have always mocked any attempts by Washington to discipline Nicaragua's politics. All past attempts to do this—and there have been many—have failed miserably.

The basic reason for this is the nature of Nicaragua's political culture as it developed over several centuries. It is uniquely different from the equalitarian and liberal Anglo-Saxon system of town-hall New England. Yankee Protestants have had a hard time understanding this, but this has not prevented them from frequent interventions into Nicaragua's internal political system.

While these historic interventions were forced by domestic revolution which threatened regional stability, the U.S. still made honest efforts to promote long-term democracy. The fact that Nicaragua wound up with a shallow stability and little true democracy reflects less on the U.S. than it does on the stubborn continuity of the political culture Nicaragua inherited from Spain in early nineteenth century Central America.

Historically, Nicaragua was more of a city-state in political culture than a nation, in the European sense of the term. About the size of New York State, with a current population of 2.5 million, its two rival political factions have warred with each other in Mafia-style infighting for well over a century. Like the Kentucky family feuds of old, Nicaragua's Machiavellian politics have been rife with coup d'état, intrigue and revolution. The system has existed that way since independence in

2

1821. Its Spanish heritage sponsored a parochial and patriarchal system of local *caudillos* who governed the conditions of Nicaragua's politics. Revolution and paternalism have been the enduring political pillars of Nicaragua, and they have defied every single North American attempt to "enlighten" them into textbook reflections of liberal American democracy. This family- and geographically-based system predated Anastasio Somoza by over 150 years.

For the first twenty years after independence from Spain, a parade of eighteen Presidents succeeded each other in coup and counter-coup. Thus, Nicaraguan political leaders began a pattern that persisted into the twentieth century. The system was based upon a near continuous warfare, gangland-style, between the Liberal and Conservative parties.

These names, however, were simply conveniences. Aside from certain class distinctions, the two parties have been mostly separated by regional differences. Granada, at the western end of Lake Nicaragua, became the power center of the Conservatives, while Liberal headquarters emerged at Leon, the largest city. The arch-rivalry of these two areas began soon after 1821, and an intense political hatred continued throughout the nineteenth century. As a symbol of neutrality, Managua became the permanent capital.

Like gang warfare, the political struggle in Nicaragua was over "turf" and spoil, rather than ideology or principle. Very few of the Indian peasants in the remote northern mountains, or the Negroes of the isolated eastern coast participated in the ongoing political wars of the two western cities. The system grew into an elitist competition between urban-based factions of mestizo (Spanish-Indian blood) clans.

These clans were the direct ancestors of the same families that made the rebellions of the twentieth century. Anastasio Somoza's great-granduncle, for example, was a famous revolutionary of the 1840's. Somoza's archenemy during the 1970's was the Conservative journalist, Pedro Joaquín Chamorro. His distant cousin, Fruto Chamarro, was President in the 1850's and founded the Conservative Party. In many ways, the rivalry of a handful of great families tells much of the history of Nicaraguan politics.

By the turn of the century, Nicaragua was under the control of the Liberal dictator, José Santa Zelaya. In retrospect, his rule was probably the tightest and most oppressive in the nation's history. His violations of human rights, as defined today, were flagrant and open. Three separate Conservative revolts were ruthlessly put down. Personal and property rights were shamelessly abandoned. Political opposition was banned; murder and torture of Conservatives grew into systematic repression.

But it was Zelaya's foreign and military policies that caught the attention of the United States. This led to his own downfall and to the first sustained America invervention in Nicaragua.

3

Zelaya turned a backward country into a military power, Central American style. He pressured the British out of the eastern coast and then occupied the entire country. He organized a strong militia and equipped it with modern machine guns. His army was the strongest in the region, and he proved it in 1907 by defeating both the Honduran and Salvadoran armies together. His adventurism by then was running directly counter to the newly-established U.S. insistence upon regional stability and peace.

The building of an interoceanic canal and the assertion of American power in the Isthmus were the two critical factors in the original U.S. interest in Nicaragua. These factors illustrate the evolving differences between the Nicaraguan and American political perspectives on Central America.

American Strategy

The American interest in Central American politics grew from the perspective of a great power with both regional and global interests. U.S. interest in construction of a canal between the seas focused early attention on a possible route through Nicaragua. From that time forward, the unequal power between the small and unstable country of the South and the "colossus of the North" took the form of an imperial-client relationship. Without a choice, Nicaragua became a pawn in this game of nineteenth century global power politics.

Geopolitics have determined Nicaragua's weakness between the great powers, just as her Spanish and Indian culture shaped her domestic political system. A *New York Times* correspondent, writing in 1928, made an important observation on this permanent feature of Nicaragua's geopolitical vulnerability:

> It has been Nicaragua's fate, often an evil fate like that of a woman too lovely, to be desired by many nations. Geological forces laid out the area which was to be Nicaragua at a point destined to be of enormous strategic importance to the great powers of the world. The existence across the territory of Nicaragua of a favorable route for a trans-Isthmian canal to join the two great seas of the world made Nicaragua a potential Gibraltar of the West which a strong nation inevitably would some day dominate.[2]

U.S. strategic interest in Nicaragua pre-dated dictator Zelaya's adventurism by half a century. Initial American concern in an interoceanic route dates back to the 1830's and slowly grew by stages during the nineteenth century. Until the late 1840's little attention was given the idea. But as U.S. continental acquisitions on the Pacific Coast developed, interest in an Isthmiam canal route heightened.

In the 1848 Bidlack Treaty with Colombia, the U.S. was guaranteed the right of way or transit across the Isthmus of Panama. This stimulated British diplomacy to secure control of the alternate Nicaraguan route to checkmate the U.S. position at Panama. The acute rivalry which then developed was compromised by the 1850 Clayton-Bulwer Treaty, which placed any future Isthmian railway or canal under the joint control of the United States and Great Britain. Each power further agreed not to fortify nor colonize the canal or its vicinity.

This compromise pleased nobody. The Clayton-Bulwer Treaty has been described as "perhaps the most unpopular treaty in the history of the United States, a big troublemaker in subsequent Anglo-American affairs."[3] The U.S. never remained satisfied with its provisions and, for half a century, U.S. policy wavered between complaining acquiescence and open defiance of its terms. Between 1849 and 1914 the United States negotiated ten separate treaties with Nicaragua regarding a canal route. In the meantime, British policy doggedly clung to the Clayton-Bulwer Treaty as the best vehicle with which to assure continuation of British maritime interests in Central America.

By the end of the Civil War, a unified America renewed more vigorously its interests in the canal site. State Department focus had by now shifted to Panama. But the Nicaraguan route was still very much alive, and in 1872 and 1876 surveys were made along the San Juan River and Lake Nicaragua. In 1878, the French conclusion of a treaty with Colombia aroused American fears. The next year President Hayes officially stated that the United States alone must construct and control any Isthmian canal.

During the early 1880's, the first direct and vigorous American efforts for release from the Clayton-Bulwer Treaty occurred. A series of notes to London cabled U.S. urgings that the treaty be cancelled. The British refused.

By the late 1890's, however, ominous developments in world politics forced Britain's hand. Of particular importance was the growing menace of Germany and England's frustration in its traditional policy of "splendid isolation." A reversal of this policy demanded allies, and the British began glancing toward the United States. British concessions to the U.S. in a 1895 Venezuela boundary dispute were a portent of events to come, as the United States, now under the spirit of "Manifest Destiny," pressed hard for strategic domination in the Caribbean Basin.

In the meantime, Congress had authorized an independent commission to investigate alternate canal routes, since both official and unofficial sentiment was still undecided. This report preferred Nicaragua *unless* and *until* the French Company's holdings in Colombia could be purchased for $40 million or less. The French company, after a series of amazing diplomatic intrigues by the French financier Philippe Bunau-Varilla, agreed to the terms, opening the door further for Panama advocates.[4]

A second stumbling block—treaty restrictions with Great Britain—was hurdled with the 1902 conclusion of the Hay-Pauncefote Treaty.

This superceded the Clayton-Bulwer Treaty by granting to the United States the sole right to build, own, and operate the canal, as well as the right of sovereign ownership and fortification over the site.

The American-sponsored "revolution" in Panama closed the deal. Private companies were still, as late as 1902, surveying the Nicaraguan route, but this ended after the official selection of Panama. Financial diplomacy and the balance of power had left Nicaragua an international bride-in-waiting.

By 1907 the effects of U.S. Manifest Destiny and British foreign policy had secured American preeminence in the Caribbean and Central America. Theodore Roosevelt's "corollary" to the Monroe Doctrine and William Howard Taft's "dollar diplomacy" were diplomatic and economic attempts to maintain U.S. strategic supremacy by precluding any further causes for potential European intervention. Chronic political instability and financial disarray were traditional pretexts for European interference into the region. In an attempt to remove these causes and to police the area, both Roosevelt and Taft then launched the era of U.S. military intervention in the Caribbean.

In Central America, Nicaragua's President Zelaya tried to force a Federal Union with himself at the head. Protests from U.S. nationals inside Nicaragua, plus requests for aid from neighboring countries, began the revolt which toppled his government and set the stage for the first U.S. military occupation of Nicaragua in 1909. International strategy and the regional balance of power forced the U.S., against its will, into military intervention.

From the end of the Spanish-American War in 1898 to the beginning of the Good Neighbor Policy in 1933, American troops made over twenty separate landings in the Caribbean and Central America. The underlying cause of these interventions was *strategic*. In toto, they reflected Washington's deep desire to restrain both internal political revolt and foreign military interference. Both objectives became twin pillars of U.S. foreign policy. The American national interest in Central America was best expressed in simple but classic terms in 1927 by Assistant Secretary of State, Robert Olds:

> Geographical facts cannot be ignored. The Central American area down to and including the Isthmus of Panama constitutes a legitimate sphere of influence for the United States; if we are to have due regard for our own safety and protection.

> Call it a sphere of influence, or what you will, we do control the destinies of Central America, and we do it for the simple reason that the national interest absolutely dictates such a course.

II. INTERVENTION AND OCCUPATION, 1909-1927

From 1912 to 1933 the United States was in occupation of Nicaragua. A U.S. military presence kept the peace, and American authorities ran the entire economic and political system. So complete was U.S. overlordship, that one commentator of the time noted that "The United States has ruled Nicaragua during the past eighteen years more completely than the American Federal Government rules any state in the Union."[5]

This twenty-one year period was a crucial time in the spectrum of relations between the two countries. It was the era that brought in Augusto C. Sandino, who led guerrillas of the northern mountains against the U.S. Marines for over five years. The era also saw the creation of the *Guardia Nacional* and its eventual control by General Anastasio Somoza García, who used it as the mechanism for a dynasty of more than four decades. Thus, the period of U.S. occupation spawned both the Somoza and the Sandinista systems, the two dominant political factions in modern Nicaragua history. The echoes of the past are still with us today.

This early-century period has been a subject of great controversy, especially with critics of U.S. policy. The legend persists that the United States was responsible for the creation of the Somoza reign, that it promoted the Somoza family deliberately and that, in effect, the U.S. sponsored dictatorship in Nicaragua. As one Nicaraguan nationalist has stated, U.S. influence was "deeply corruptive of Nicaragua's public morale," and the hold over the country by the Somoza government was "closely linked to the political intervention of the United States."[6] In other words, the U.S. was to blame for the lack of political democracy in Nicaraguan history. Latin American nationalists and liberal U.S. academics have a strange alliance on this issue.

History, however, is a bit more complicated than that. The story of the U.S. occupation of Nicaragua will unfold a series of painful and

7

reluctant American interventions against a background of Nicaraguan political chaos, violence and revolution. The intrigues of the battling Conservatives and Liberals of Nicaragua played an important part in U.S. interventions. The party in power, in fact, used U.S. troops to keep the other party down, while the U.S. viewed its occupation as a necessary nuisance against chronic wrongdoing in Nicaragua. What happened subsequently was in large part the result of historic accident: the clash of two political systems with vastly different perspectives and outlooks.

The first military contact between the U.S. and Nicaragua was not even sanctioned by the American government. In 1855, a young Californian mercenary and journalist, William Walker, was persuaded by the Liberal Party to help finance and organize a revolt against the Conservative government. Walker's "army" of about sixty other adventurers, helped by southern U.S. politicians who wanted Nicaragua as a slave state, succeeded in defeating the Conservative Army easily. The next year Walker had himself named as President, declared English as the language of the country and officially reinstated slavery. He then set about a conquest of the rest of Central America, a venture which put him in front of a Honduran firing squad in 1860, thus ending this "mouse that roared" comic-opera.

Between the end of the Walker episode and the beginnings of the Zelaya regime in 1893, contacts between the U.S. and Nicaragua were largely confined to the canal issue. It wasn't until Zelaya began to exceed his boundaries that the U.S. became involved.

The American military intervention of 1909, and subsequent occupation of Nicaragua, however, was never undertaken enthusiastically and was forced by events in the region over which Washington had little or no control. The excesses of President Zelaya against his own citizens and against his neighbors finally forced the U.S. government to take a firm hand against the political turbulence then unfolding in Nicaragua and Central America. Ironically, against his will also, Zelaya himself was responsible for the American occupation.

The First Intervention

By 1909 Washington had become thoroughly irritated with Zelaya's government and, like the rest of Central America, was looking for ways to get rid of him. The United States was prepared to assist a rebellion against him, but it would take three years before full military intervention would be used as the last-straw alternative. Between 1909 and 1912 the U.S. alternatively flirted with diplomatic persuasion and restrained military force to secure a change. Having failed that, the United States reluctantly intervened in full in 1912.

8

The revolution against Zelaya began in 1909 in Bluefields on the eastern coast. Although nominally led by a Liberal, the revolution was organized mostly by Conservatives. The American settlement living in Nicaragua openly sided with the rebels, while businessmen in the United States put up $1 million to help finance the revolution. Almost at once the Conservatives established a coalition government at Bluefields under the provisional presidency of Juan J. Estrada, an anti-Zelaya Liberal. Washington then broke relations with the Zelaya regime, the Secretary of State accusing him in an official letter of having "almost continually kept Central America in tension or turmoil."

During the summer of 1909 U.S. Marines were dispatched to Bluefields, ostensibly to protect lives and property. With the approach of Zelaya's army, however, the Marines secured the town for the rebels to use as a sanctuary. By December 1909 Zelaya's days were numbered. The lack of American recognition and the realization that he could not win militarily forced his resignation in favor of another member of the Liberal Party.

But Washington still refused recognition, and the war was renewed. By early 1910 the rebels were once again pushed back into Bluefields, where a force of 400 Marines provided a Conservative sanctuary. Prevented again from crushing their opponents by American military power, the Liberals resigned the Presidency for good in August 1910. For the second time in less than a year, the mere presence of U.S. Marines in Nicaragua's isolated east coast was enough to change the government in Managua. The Americans, so far, had yet to fire a shot.

With all vestiges of Zelaya gone, the rebels assumed power. General Estrada became president and promised to hold free elections within two years. The United States took over Nicaragua's economy, lock, stock and barrel. Through a series of arrangements negotiated by U.S. financial agents, the United States undertook all economic claims against Nicaragua. By mid-year 1911 the U.S. had secured a loan of $1.5 million and was in control of Nicaragua's customs. The country's foreign debt was refunded, the currency was stabilized, and tax laws were regulated according to Washington's desires. With a stable economy, the country appeared to be getting back on its feet after the ravages of civil war. U.S. intervention seemed a success.

The historic political antagonism between Liberals and Conservatives, however, once more threatened Washington's cherished stability. The 1910 revolution, although led by a Liberal, had the basis of its support in the Conservative Party. With only one exception (the Minister of Government), Estrada's coalition government was Conservative. In spite of that, Minister of War Luis Mena, another Conservative, went after the Liberal president Estrada with a vengenance characteristic of the country's traditional political hatreds. With Mena in control

9

of the armed forces, there was little the Liberals could do to prevent a Conservative takeover.

By May 1911 Estrada was forced out in a coup d'etat. The new president, the third chief executive in eighteen months, was Adolpho Díaz, Conservative Vice President of the brief Estrada regime. Díaz received prompt U.S. recognition, as it appeared at last that a formula had been found to keep the lid on Nicaragua's chronic political instability. The worst was yet to come.

Within the next year, U.S. officials reluctantly concluded that only full military intervention could halt the chaotic parade of Nicaraguan political events. Once again the culprit was Minister of War Mena, the same individual who was responsible for Díaz' succession to the presidency in the first place. Restless under Díaz, Mena decided by 1912 that his only chance for power was to launch another revolution. In July, Mena's followers in the Army attacked the government's garrison at La Loma. Liberal forces then joined Mena at the town of Masaya, in what soon became a renewed version of the 1909 civil war. Again, the State Department became alarmed. When President Díaz requested American intervention to protect his threatened regime, the request was granted immediately.

In August 1912 Major Smedley Butler landed at Corinto at the head of a Marine battalion and proceeded directly to Managua. Shortly afterwards another American force landed at Bluefields. By October, American military strength had reached a peak of 2,700 men. Major Butler led part of his battalion to Granada where he forced General Mena to surrender. On direct instructions from President Woodrow Wilson, Marine units then attacked the remaining Liberal forces near Masaya and, in a brief skirmish, routed them at dawn in time for the Marines to return to camp for breakfast.

This battle—if it can be called that—was the only important military clash between the U.S. and Nicaraguan government troops during the entire period of U.S. occupation. With the civil war officially over, most of the Marines went home. For the next thirteen years a Legation Guard of 100 troops served to remind Nicaragua of the hovering presence of American financial and military power. The peace was kept, but it was kept by American bayonets.

In retrospect, this first intervention was critical in future relations between Nicaragua and the United States. Several important factors which had lasting effects between the two countries first emerged in the aftermath of the 1912 intervention. The fixed objective of order and stability became a dominant feature of American policy. Washington grew dependent upon the dominant party to provide this stability, which in that period was the Conservative Party. The Conservatives, in turn, relied upon the United States to support and to justify their continued hold on the politics of the country. The Liberals quite naturally viewed

10

U.S. policy with great suspicion, although they were just as eager as the Conservatives to own American favor. Washington, in effect, became Nicaragua's political broker, and became the dominant actor in the domestic political system.

As unofficial overseer of the political system of Nicaragua, the United States began devising ways for the country to adopt a democratic political system. U.S. officials grew firm in their belief that only a true democracy, with free elections, could produce permanent political stability. This produced an inherent political contradiction in U.S. policy. Thus, the U.S. began demanding both stability and democracy in Nicaragua, political goals which had been mutually exclusive throughout the country's history. Eventually, one would have to to go.

U.S. discomfiture with Nicaragua's political style was understandable. So was Washington's unquestioning confidence in the universality of liberal and democratic political values. In the long run this led to an unrealistic assessment of the effects which American brokerage could have upon the local political culture.

Washington viewed its occupation of the country as a necessary evil, an embarrassment that would have to be endured until the time when Nicaragua could permanently adopt American political ways. Only when Nicaragua matured to full democracy, Washington felt, could the Marines afford to leave. Stability, in effect, was equated with democratic political methods. Nothing else would suffice.

During the occupation the United States successfully promoted the presidency of Conservative Emiliano Chamorro in 1916, only to be dismayed when he attempted to skirt the constitution by running again in 1920. Blocked by the State Department, Chamorro connived instead to install his uncle, Diego Chamorro, as president, and for himself he grabbed the country's number two political post: Minister to Washington.

Undaunted, the U.S. dispatched Dr. Harold Dodds of Princeton University to Nicaragua in order to draft a new electoral law for the country. Sentiment in the United States, especially in liberal and academic circles, was pressing for a withdrawal of the Marines. The Dodds electoral reforms provided hope that force would not be needed again.

The American-drafted election law passed its first test in 1924 with flying colors. Special pains were taken to ensure fairness, including outside supervision in each of the country's fourteen districts. The coalition ticket headed by the Conservative Party's candidate, Carlos Solórzano, won decisively in the fairest election in Nicaraguan history to that date. Plans were made to withdraw the U.S. Legation Guard. Democracy had come to Nicaragua, or so it seemed.

Less than a year later, however, political anarchy and violence returned to Nicaragua in what was to be the bloodiest period of the country's history (until 1978). The eventual U.S. response to the 1926

11

civil war was a redoubled effort to install political democracy and stability in Nicaragua at all costs. This soon committed U.S. Marines in a protracted war against the guerrilla forces of Augusto C. Sandino, a contest that went on for nearly six years, with no final result except to instill in the State Department a sober pessimism as to the U.S. ability to remake the Nicaraguan political character. This era also began the domination of the country by the American-created *Guardia Nacional* and its first Nicaraguan *Jefe Director,* Anastasio Somoza García.

The Second Intervention

The violence of the late 1920's opens another page in Nicaraguan-U.S. relations. To a certain extent, the withdrawal of the Marines in 1925 was governed by an optimism regarding the character of *international* politics, almost as much as it was regarding Nicaraguan politics. The main motivations of the early-century interventions was the fear of instability in an area so close to the Panama Canal and, likewise, of the effects which such instability would have on possible outside intervention in Central America. After the defeat of Germany in 1918, plus better relations with Britain and Japan, this traditional American vigilance was no longer necessary. With a relatively safe international environment, plus what it thought were good prospects for democracy and financial stability in Nicaragua, Washington pulled the Legation Guard out.

In the place of the Marines, the U.S. left a new military force: the *Guardia Nacional de Nicaragua* (National Guard). The creation of this body, in retrospect, was one of the key decisions made by U.S. officials in the long history of involvement with Nicaragua.

The establishment of non-partisan costabularies in the states of the Caribbean area was a long-standing policy of the U.S. The older armies, as in Nicaragua, were viewed as the main causes of the disorder, graft and revolution which prevailed almost everywhere. As personal armies of the regime in power, they became the mainstays of Caribbean dictatorships. When revolts ensued, they also began within the army. As a force for stability, therefore, military politics in the Caribbean were inherently unhealthy. The American objective in Haiti, the Dominican Republic and elsewhere was to replace these armies with disciplined constabularies, trained by U.S. officers, recruited from all segments of the populace and loyal to the nation as a whole, not to the regime.

In 1925 the U.S. prevailed upon the Nicaraguan government to form a constabulary to replace both the old Army and the Marines. The final legislation creating the *Guardia*, however, was not exactly what Washington wanted. From the very beginnings, the Nicaraguan government did its level best to assure that the *Guardia* would reflect the wishes of the regime in power. President Solórzano kept control over important functions of the new force, as did all of his successors. At the start, the *Guardia Nacional* was an American invention, forced upon a reluctant Nicaraguan government as a U.S. device to promote non-partisan stability. In reality, the exact opposite took place.

By the time the Legation Guard of Marines departed, in August 1925, the new *Guardia* had a skeleton force of 250 officers and men. Major Calvin B. Carter was sent down as the first U.S. director. Within weeks of his arrival, however, a new political crisis began another round of revolutionary violence, dashing optimistic American hopes for Nicaraguan stability, and for the future of a truly nonpartisan *Guardia*.

The violence of 1926-27 was worse than before. The fundamental cause was nearly an exact repetition of the troubles which preceded the 1912 intervention. The same root factors were present: perscnalism and factionalism in the military, the historic antagonism between Liberals and Conservatives, the instinctive will to revolt, and the elitist jealousy among the several great families of both parties which historically have vied for power in Nicaragua's turbulent political system.

Almost immediately after the departure of the Marines, President Solórzano found his position assaulted by General Chamorro, who controlled the Conservative press. At 2 A.M. on October 25, his followers surrounded the President's home. Chamorro was named Commander of the Army and control of the country passed into his hands. Liberals throughout the government were then systematically purged and, in March 1926, the Nicaraguan Congress accepted Solórzano's resignation, with Chamorro formally replacing him as President. Like many presidents before him, his reign was to be short and violent.

The inevitable Liberal uprising began, typically, in Bluefields in May 1926. After assuming command of the *Guardia*, Chamorro went after the Liberals in force. Early setbacks failed to still Liberal enthusiasm, however, and the revolt continued throughout the summer and fall of 1926. By early 1927 the Liberals were beginning to win, but the prolonged violence had begun to take its toll on the country. Armed bands of deserters from both sides were terrorizing the population. Crops were left fallow, and famine hit all sections of the country.

The State Department had refused recognition of Chamorro's coup and, throughout most of the year, it had urged his resignation. As before, the lack of American support became the determinant, and in October 1926 Chamorro resigned in favor of Adolfo Díaz, another Conservative. American support for Díaz, once again, was near automatic, but it was prompted this time by an entirely new element in the picture: the fear of Mexican encroachment in the civil war and the perceived replacement of American influence in the Central American Isthmus.

Washington was still sensitive to disruptions in the Caribbean region and in Central America, even through Europe was no longer a threat.

13

The specter of Mexican influence now haunted Washington and moved the United States closer to a second intervention and closer to the faction inside Nicaragua which would provide the greatest degree of political stability. For the moment, that faction continued to be Adolfo Díaz and the Conservative Party.

Relations between the U.S. and Mexico had been strained for many years. The 1910 revolution in Mexico was nationalistic and politically leftward, and the military intervention undertaken by President Wilson in 1916 had still not been forgotten by the Mexican government. Many Americans believed that Mexico was dominated by "Bolshevism," and there were genuine fears inside the State Department that Mexico was out to challenge the U.S. in its Central American hegemony. When the Nicaraguan fighting began again in 1926, Mexico openly favored the Liberals, and arms shipments from Mexican ports had, in fact, reached the rebels and had helped sustain their war effort. Referring to Mexico, President Coolidge told Congress in January 1927:

I have the most conclusive evidence that arms and munitions in large quantities have been, on several occasions since August 1926, shipped to the revolutionists in Nicaragua . . . The United States cannot fail to view with deep concern any serious threat to stability and constitutional government in Nicaragua tending toward anarchy and jeopardizing American interests, especially if such a state of affairs is contributed to or brought about by outside influence or by a foreign power.

Within two months the United States was back in Nicaragua in force. By the spring of 1927 over 2,000 Marines had landed, and Washington was openly supplying the Díaz regime with arms and material. Whatever reality the Mexican threat had, it was over as fast as it had arisen. Nevertheless, the civil war, now effectively a military stalemate, dragged on.

American policy then moved to end the country's chronic violence and disorder once and for all. The President dispatched Henry L. Stimson, a prominent Republican and former Secretary of War under William H. Taft, to negotiate an end to the conflict and to stabilize the political system for good. In May, Stimson ended the rebellion with the threat of American force, and promised U.S. help in the formation of another Guardia and U.S. supervision of new elections. By June more Marines arrived, pushing the total to over 3,000.

For the second time in a generation the United States had taken almost complete control of Nicaragua in a search for the right combination of political order and democracy. This second test was to be a failure more lasting than the first and, before it was finished, it not only produced an endless and frustrating guerrilla war against the Sandinistas, but it also effectively removed the United States from the business of political overseer of Latin American countries.

14

In Nicaragua, the second American intervention recreated the vehicle for the rise to power of the Somoza family (the *Guardia Nacional*) and laid the basis for U.S. policy to court President Somoza, the Liberal Party and the stability which they brought to the country. In effect, U.S. policy reversed itself almost 180 degrees. By the end of the Sandino War in 1933, Washington was through with intervention and was seeking political stability at almost any price.

The Stimson mission ended in June 1927 with U.S. Marines dispersed throughout Nicaragua, disarming all those who still wished to pursue the civil war. With one important exception, the Marines succeeded.

Augusto C. Sandino was a comparatively little-known Liberal soldier with a history of nationalistic and anti-American political activism. In July he retreated to the northern mountains with about 300 armed sympathizers and refused to surrender. For the next five and one-half years he and his followers waged a classic guerrilla war against a dual foe: the government in Managua and the American Marines.

This war was quickly forgotten north of Mexico, but not in Latin America. In the turmoil of today's guerrilla wars in Central America, few Americans will recall the original. But the frustrations of fighting Sandino's peasant and Indian partisans had an important affect upon over four decades of U.S. foreign policy. Its immediate impact was the Somoza dynasty; its ultimate effect still remains to be felt, as Sandino's heirs have now taken the throne.

III. SANDINO AND THE SANDINISTAS, 1921-33

The campaign by the U.S. Marines to destroy the first Sandinista movement was a crucial determinant for U.S.—Nicaraguan relations. In Nicaragua, it was a watershed between U.S. occupation and the Somoza dynasty. To all classes of modern-day Nicaraguans, Sandino had been a household word, for good or bad, decades before the American media discovered a romantic defiance in the groups of youth that made up the second generation of Sandinistas.

To the regime now in power in Nicaragua, Augusto Sandino is a patron saint. His anti-Americanism and his generic blend of mestizo nationalism and socialist economics makes Sandino the ideological godfather of the present government. He was Nicaragua's Che Guevara. He fought both the Yankees and the politicians in Managua and, like Guevara, he was a martyr to the cause. In Nicaragua today, Sandino is the official hero of the nation. To the U.S. State Department in the 1930's, he was a "bandit." To most Americans today, he is still unknown, a mystery at best. Who was this "Quixote on a Burro," whose name and spirit now hovers over contemporary Nicaragua?

Augusto César Sandino[7] was born on May 18, 1895, in the village of Niquinihomo in the department of Masaya. His father was an active Liberal *político* and a small plantation owner. Sandino went to primary school and later became a merchant and small landowner. During his adolescence, he went to school with Anastasio Somoza García.

In 1921, Sandino left Nicaragua to live in Honduras, Guatemala, and Mexico. With his half-brother, Sócrates, he worked at a sugar plantation in Honduras, but in 1922 he was forced to leave the country after a quarrel with the local authorities. In Guatemala, he worked at United Fruit, where he became acquainted with the workers' grievances against U.S. "imperialism." It was here that he began a conversion to socialism and Central American nationalism against the economic domination of the United States.

17

In the 1920's, Mexico was home to a variety of radical political movements, particularly syndicalist and communist groups. In 1923, the restless wanderer Sandino moved to Mexico to work for an American petroleum company in Tampico. In Mexico, Sandino developed into a true revolutionary.

Without higher education, Sandino became influenced by Mexican nationalists and Central American political exiles who schooled him on social problems, theology and economics. He studied the tactics of labor leaders and gradually evolved his own combination of Nicaraguan nationalism and socialism. He was reminded, caustically, of the American domination of Nicaragua. He discovered that his purpose and destiny, therefore, was to resurrect sovereignty to his home country against U.S. overlordship. In 1926, the civil war in Nicaragua threatened a second American military intervention. Sandino left Mexico and headed for home, now dedicated fanatically to his new-found purpose.

Back home, Sandino found an outlet for his dedication at the U.S.-owned San Albino gold mine. Employed as a timekeeper, he spent most of his energy agitating the miners to the need for social reform. His anti-establishment instincts made him begin a political movement independent of either the Liberals or the Conservatives. With his entire savings of three hundred dollars, he bought arms in Honduras and equipped a band of twenty-nine men in the northern province of Nueva Segovia, October 1926. The *Sandinistas,* thus, were born.

Sandinism in the 1920's

A military defeat in November against the government, however, quickly forced Sandino to abandon his independence and to join the Liberal cause. His band was merged into an army led by José M. Moncada, who would become President in 1928.

From the beginnings, neither Moncada—the established Liberal—nor Sandino—the radical guerrilla—trusted one another. This mistrust later grew into bitter hatred when Moncada's government, backed by 5,000 U.S. Marines, waged war against Sandino's men. The subsequent relationship between Moncada and Sandino is of great importance as a major factor in the continuation of the guerrilla war of 1927-33.

When the civil war was winding down in May 1927, U.S. emissary Henry L. Stimson and Moncada negotiated a truce at the village of Tipitapa. Sandino viewed the negotiations with great suspicion, and on several occasions publicly accused Moncada of selling out to the Americans. He even believed that Moncada had maneuvered the Liberal army into surrender, in order to promote his own presidential ambitions. To Sandino, Moncada was an American puppet.

In the war council, Sandino vehemently opposed the truce and argued for a general uprising against the U.S. To placate him, Moncada offered Sandino the governorship of Jinotega province, but this effort failed.

18

Sandino was beyond compromise; he wanted both revolution and power. Of all the Liberal leaders in the civil war, he was the only one who refused to meet the U.S. terms for disarmament and for supervised elections in 1928. Sandino considered both traitorous. *"Mueran los Yanquis"* ("Death to the Yankees") became his battle cry.

As soon as the truce document was signed, Sandino and his followers slipped away from Moncada to a remote area of the north. In San Rafael del Norte, the guerrilla leaders prepared to evict the Americans with three hundred armed men.

Moncada quickly understood the significance of Sandino's move. He enlisted the aid of Sandino's father, and personally accompanied the Marines to call upon Sandino to disarm. This summons provoked an argument among Sandino's followers. Desertions increased, and within days he was left with only thirty men. Sandino then retreated to the Honduran border town of Yali. It was in Yali that his father, Don Gregorio, attempted to dissuade Sandino from further resistance. The conference with his father, however, only resulted in the conversion of Don Gregorio to his son's cause.

Sandino now understood that Moncada was as great an enemy to his revolution as the Americans were. His subsequent war was waged against *all* his enemies, the foreigners in Marine uniforms and the politicians in the capital, both Liberal and Conservative.

Throughout the arduous guerrilla campaign that followed, both the Nicaraguan and Washington governments variously classified Sandino as a "bandit" or "outlaw." When the Marines withdrew in January 1933, at the time Sandino's armed resistance ceased, the official classification of Sandino as a bandit was still in force. By attacking U.S.-owned property and by clinging to the traditional revolutionary practice of looting, Sandino—to be sure—gave substance to these charges. But the credibility of this official view has to be judged against Sandino's unflinching opposition to Moncada, his own revolutionary ardor and the fixed and historic American objectives in Nicaragua.

U.S. denunciation of Sandino as a bandit was motivated by its desire to convince the American public and the world that the United States was intervening in Nicaragua to preserve order and peace against illegal and vicious outlawry. With the civil war officially over, the United States refused to recognize the existence of a revolutionary third party in Nicaragua. The charges of banditry had become a U.S. effort against official recognition of the Sandinistas as a political party in Nicaragua. The U.S. was badly misled.

The U.S. was also misled on the early nature of Sandino's military strength. During the month of June, Sandino had again built up his forces to several hundred, and had retired further into the remote mountains of the north. The Stimson mission, however, was ended optimistically. Stimson cabled home that "there will be no organized resistance to our action." He also wrote that there was "less danger of banditry and guerrilla warfare than I at first feared." The U.S. command in Managua predicted that Sandino would be "annihilated."

Sandino barely allowed the Marines sufficient time to organize. In the early hours of July 16, he launched his men, armed with small arms and machetes, against the town of Ocotal in northwest Nicaragua. Ocotal was being defended by 87 Marines plus *Guardia*. After two open exchanges, the defenders were driven back into several fortified buildings in the town. With ammunition running low, and with communications cut off, the Marines found themselves in a deadly position.

In mid-morning, however, rescue came from an unusual place: the sky. Two roaming U.S. biplanes happened upon the scene by accident. They quickly flew back to Managua. Hours later, a squadron of five American de Haviland bombers returned with a vengeance. As the Sandinistas fled from the planes, they were cut down repeatedly with small bombs and machine guns.

History's first known dive bombing attack in support of ground troops produced an appalling result. At least two hundred Sandinistas were reported dead. The Marines lost only one man, but the planes saved them all.[8] Major E. H. Brainard, who took part in the battle, testified to Congress that "if the planes had not brought immediate assistance, there is no question but the whole band would have been slaughtered."

The battle of Ocotal is the single most important military event in U.S.-Nicaraguan history, prior to the 1978-79 civil war. After such a staggering defeat, Sandino thereafter refused to fight the Marines directly. For the next several years, he moved, quickly and at will, with hundreds of men, in a classic guerrilla war in the dense mountains of northern Nicaragua.

Ocotal also brought the issue to the rest of the world. News of the massacre spread fast and far. Sandino's prestige soared, domestic criticism in the U.S. mounted, as the American command found it embarrassingly difficult to explain its growing predicaments against peasant "bandits." It soon became impossible to explain the fiction of banditry in the face of an increasingly popular Sandinista movement.

Indeed, the emergence of the Sandinistas as a political force beyond the borders of Nicaragua was as important as their military activities inside the country. Sandinism was an international phenomenon in the 1920's and '30's just as it was in the 1970's. Much of Sandino's international prestige was a direct outgrowth of Ocotal and the subsequent elusive guerrilla campaign he waged against the Marines. Like Fidel Castro, Che Guevara and Commander "Zero" of a later generation, Augusto Sandino was a romantic folk-hero, a political Robin Hood to the international left-wing of the 1920's.

His cause was taken up throughout the Latin American left: by Argentina's socialist leader Alfredo Palacios, the Chilean poet Gabriela

Mistral, the Mexican intellectual José Vasconcelos, the Peruvian revolutionary Victor Raul Haya de la Torre, etc. He was also seized upon
by anti-U.S. governments in Latin America as a *cause celebre* against
growing U.S. influence.

The international reaction to U.S. intervention was almost universally hostile, particularly in Latin America. This was a regional movement, led by the Argentine government, and came to be much more
than student and left-wing posturing. The second Marine intervention
in Nicaragua happened to coincide with the emergence of an era of
protest in Latin America against the continuing interference of the U.S.
in Central America. The Sandino War became the focal point for this
discontent. Throughout the entire episode, the Latin American press
was nearly unanimous in its emphatic and constant denunciations of the
never-ending U.S. war against the Sandinistas.

At the Sixth Pan American Conference in 1928, the Nicaraguan intervention became the lead topic. U.S. diplomats were placed on the
defensive for the first time in history. Resolutions against Washington
filled the air. Besides the Nicaraguan government, only Haiti and Cuba
(both occupied by U.S. forces) defended Washington. Indeed, the Sandino affair was the immediate prelude to the non-interventionist foreign
policies pursued by the Roosevelt Administration.

The European reaction to the United States intérvention was aloof
and much more gentile, but hardly more sympathetic. Europe, as a
whole, viewed the American difficulties with amused sarcasm. The
intervention, however, according to the *New York Times,* "caused
more discussion in Europe than any action by Washington since the
rejection of the Treaty of Versailles."[9] American incursions into Nicaragua were thought to have "brought many chuckles in England,
France, Germany, and Italy . . .[since, Europe felt] the United States
has put herself on record in a fashion which will bind her to silence
when the occasion presents itself to European powers to take analogous
steps where their interests are at stake."[10] With her vast colonial
empires in mind, Europe tactfully reminded America to mind its own
business.

The early Sandinistas were crude but effective in exploiting this anti-
U.S. feeling. Sandinista propaganda agents distributed literature
throughout the western hemisphere and many of the leading newspapers
regularly printed pro-Sandino statements. Sandino's propaganda arm
regularly emphasized the themes of Hispanic nationalism and anti-
Americanism and customarily exaggerated the success of his military
operations against the Marines. His movement was given wide coverage
and, in reality, represented a hemispheric propaganda war much greater
in proportion than Sandino's actual military success within Nicaragua.
In retrospect, Sandino's agents in the western hemisphere were original
versions of a Latin American *"internationale."*

21

His propaganda network was widespread. In Guatemala there was "Cigarrillo Sandino," while "Nectar Sandino," a liquor, was sold in El Salvador. There was a Sandino Division in the Russian-advised Nanking Army during the 1927 Chinese Civil War. Toribio Tijerino, one of Sandino's propagandists, started a new Central American publication called *Sandino*, explaining the ideals and goals of Sandinism. Demonstrations, lectures, and appeals for support were common in Central America and Mexico. Many of these were sponsored by Communist and Marxist groups, such as the "Hands off Nicaragua" committee, one of at least a dozen such groups which existed in Mexico alone.

The organizational chief for much of Sandino's propaganda was Pedro Zepeda, who used Mexico as a base to circulate a flood of Sandinista literature to Latin America. José Gonzales represented Sandino at the Second World Congress of Anti-Imperialists held at Frankfurt, Germany, in July 1929. The "All American Anti-Imperialist League" in the United States circulated "Sandino" stamps until they were suppressed by the Postmaster General. Subscription drives for funds to be sent to Sandino were made both in Latin America and the United States. His brother Sócrates became a Communist party member and solicited funds inside the United States.

The Communist International originally backed his cause, and editorials in *The Daily Worker* solicited aid for him and encouraged support for the "All-American Anti-Imperialist League." But Sandino was not a party member, and during this trip to Mexico in 1929 the Communist Party, apparently convinced that he was too nationalistic for them, labeled him a "traitor to the cause." He remained, to the end, a home-inspired revolutionary.

The propaganda arms of the Sandinista movement were certainly not anticipated by American authorities. But the emergence of Sandino as an international figure quickened efforts to eliminate him. The Assistant Secretary of State, for example, wrote that: "He is . . . a figure of great international importance, especially in Latin America, and the inability of the Marines to get him so far has increased his international nuisance value and is causing us considerable annoyance in many ways."

A large part of Sandino's propaganda activity attempted to materially aid his military operations inside Nicaragua. The attempt to solicit funds, arms, food, and medical supplies was continent-wide. Early speculation as to the amount and degree of this aid was rampant, but it was nearly impossible to be precise. The following exchange in the United States Senate is illustrative:

Senator Johnson. In your opinion is he receiving any outside aid?

General Lane. There are reports to that effect, and in my opinion he is; but it is just surmise. . . .

Senator Johnson. Do you know when Sandino has received any other aid from outside countries?

Admiral Latimer. He had not when I left there, and I doubt whether he has since, except what he got from individuals across the border; not from any government.

While no Latin American government officially aided Sandino, a considerable amount of supplies were privately purchased by the guerrillas in the United States and in Latin America during the last three years of the campaign. Many boatloads of munitions reached Sandino from Mexico. Other sources of arms were either stolen or captured from Marines and *Guardia,* or given to the guerrillas by *Guardia* deserters. The American Minister to Honduras wired in 1930 that, "Honduras is used probably more than any other Central American country through which Sandino and the bandit leaders receive arms . . . but this trade is very difficult to control."

Sandino and U.S. Policy

Sandino's popularity in Latin America certainly exceeded that which he enjoyed within Nicaragua itself. His following in the country was largely confined to the peasants and Indians in the areas where his guerrilla armies roamed freely. U.S. Minister Matthew Hanna even noted that, "he is less dangerous in Nicaragua than outside of this country." But in Nueva Segovia and the other provinces patrolled by Sandinistas he had virtually unanimous support, enforced through a combination of terror and propaganda against the Marine presence. The sparsely inhabited sections of both Nicaragua and Honduras were almost exclusively Sandino territory. This contributed in a large degree to the Marine inability to eliminate him. An official communique of 1930 summarized Marine frustrations:

The natives throughout the countryside—through fear, oftentimes blood relationship to bandits, resentment at presence of U.S. forces, and in some cases an ignorant sympathy for the perverted propaganda of the bandit leaders—seldom give timely information on bandits and their movements, but on the other hand, aid and assist and forewarn bandit groups of movements of Marine and Guardia patrols.

Although the vast majority of the country's 600,000 inhabitants—living in the urban and settled areas—had little sympathy with Sandino, the Marine presence was not universally appreciated either. Exact figures as to the feelings of the average Nicaraguan (outside the guerrilla zones) are, of course, non-existent. Much of the Nicaraguan elite opinion, however, interpreted the American occupation in light of their own characteristic political wars with the opposition party. This was initially true of the Conservative majority in the House of Deputies who on several occasions temporarily blocked passage of the Guardia and Electoral Bills.

But on no occasion did the political opposition indicate serious hostility in principle to either U.S. electoral supervision or to the military campaign in the north. This was reflected in the attitude of both the Liberal and Conservative press. In 1928, Marine General Lejeune cabled that, "there is no newspaper that advocates the withdrawal of the Marines and I could find no evidence of any substantial person who advocates it."

But as the guerrilla campaign continued without significant success, many Nicaraguans grew restless under American occupation. President Moncada and leaders of the Liberal Party began to agitate for the establishment of a "National Army"—as opposed to the Marines and *Guardia*—to carry the campaign to Sandino.

For the next two years important segments of the Liberal press would frequently advocate the creation of some type of "Home Army." Much of the criticism appeared in the form of newspaper attacks on Marine efforts. In 1931, Assistant Secretary of State White wrote: "I have been somewhat concerned recently at the attacks that the Liberal press in Nicaragua appears to be making against our Marine forces . . . I am told that there seems to be a rather systematic attempt on the part of the Liberal press . . . to discredit the Marines."

The Conservative press, however, was generally quiet on this point due, Minister Hanna wrote, to "the genuine fear which exists among Conservative leaders that a *national* army would be an instrument for committing wholesale outrages against Conservatives. . . ." Here, as before, the Nicaraguan instinct was to preserve power against the political opposition by using the Army. The U.S., on the other hand, kept insisting upon an apolitical military. In Nicaragua, this was impossible.

When it was apparent that the Marines were going to leave permanently, Nicaraguan opinion was mixed. "As is perfectly natural," wrote Minister Hanna, "many people look upon the departure of the Marines with a certain amount of trepidation. This is true of the leaders of both parties and of the foreign residents. That the presence of the Marines has been a stabilizing factors has been the feeling of these people. . . ." But, he went on,

there is another side to the matter. Nicaraguans have their natural pride. . .and however much they may have welcomed the Marines in the past and recognized that their presence was necessary to the peace and welfare of the Republic, they looked toward the day when Nicaragua might be able to stand on her own feet without the assistance of the Marines.

It was futile, however, for the State Department to assure the American people and the world that the Marines had achieved a victory over Sandino and could now complacently withdraw. Sandino's publicity had made him a much more important figure in Latin America than in his homeland. While his own publicity had cast him as a patriot of sincerity and conviction, U.S. and Latin publicists, and Sandino's personal agents portrayed him as a benevolent man goaded to revolt against the tyranny of corrupt politicians and brutal foreign invasion. Sandino shrewdly played upon the sentimental sympathy of the American public for the "oppressed" by appeals for medical and other assistance. To justify his looting of the properties of foreigners, he claimed that it was a device to compel American capitalists to treat Nicaraguans equally.

But Sandino, his ideological affirmations aside, was not beyond shrewd and ambitious compromise. He was still a politico at the core, in the *caudillo* tradition. He spent most of 1929 in Mexico trying to arrange a political alliance with Mexican President Portez Gil. After frustrating delays and postponements, Sandino was rushed in and out of the President's office, empty-handed. His first attempt at regional "diplomacy" had failed abjectly.

Back in Nicaragua, Sandino promised to postpone his guerrilla revolution against the government, in favor of Vice President Aguado's attempt at a secret coup against President Moncada. This, too, failed, as did Sandino's other attempts to control the northern areas for his own forces, while leaving the southern districts to the Managua government. He even diluted his original pronouncements against a complete Marine withdrawal, versus a new demand (in 1930) that they vacate *only* the southern districts, leaving the Sandinistas in control of the north.

These machinations were not lost on Anastasio Somoza and the *Guardia Nacional*, who understood Sandino as a dangerous rival *caudillo* of the North. In the end, it was politics in Nicaragua, writ large, that determined the future of both aspirants to power.

The terrorism which Sandino conducted against the Indian peasants of the north was also largely overlooked by the public romanticism of his rebellion. Yet it is a fact that he, along with deputies such as Pedro Altamirano, Carlos Salgado and Miguel Angel Ortiz used threat, murder and repression to enlist peasants to the cause.

As the campaign dragged on, Sandino grew even more serious and deadly. Some of his lieutenants became relentless killers against both opposition and neutrals alike. The phrase *"que sea pasado por las armas"* (execute him) became a common ending of Sandino's circulars and letters.

The official Sandinista death came by machete—a much slower and torturous method than the firing squad. Minor offenses were also treated with this same instrument. These ranged from multilations to grotesque *"cortes"* which caused death by prolonged suffering. The most notorious of these was the *"corte de cumbo"*, wherein the victim's head was severed at the top by a machete, leaving the base of the brain exposed. His death took long minutes, during which he usually spun around helpless like a headless chicken.

Even slower was the *"corte de chaleco"* (waist-coat cut), where two slashes severed arm from shoulder while a third cut disemboweled the victim. Often the final blow beheaded the condemned in one stroke,

25

ending his agony instantly. "Freedom is not conquered with flowers," Sandino wrote, "but with bullets, and that is why we have had to resort to the *cortes*."

The violence of the first Sandinistas was terrorism without mercy to the natives of northern Nicaragua and to those foreigners who lived away from the protected areas. During the years 1926 through 1937 a virtual civil war tore apart the fabric of Nicaraguan society, despite the end of formal hostilities between Liberals and Conservatives in 1927. The original Sandinistas did not take power, but they came very close. That story involves the guerrilla insurrection which Augusto Sandino led against the Marines and the government between 1927 and 1933.

IV. GUERRILLA WAR: MARINES vs. SANDINISTAS, 1927-1933

"Counterinsurgency" was introduced to the U.S. public during the Vietnam War as a novel and unique form of combat for the American soldier. Unbeknown to most Americans, however, the Marine Corps practiced an earlier version of counterinsurgency in the protracted guerrilla war against the original Sandinistas. This "mini-Vietnam" has been conveniently forgotten in this country, but it is widely remembered south of the border.

Guerrilla wars have never been popular with the U.S. public, especially ones that don't win. In a political sense, the U.S. "lost" the Sandino war despite the huge disparity in military strength. This interesting episode became the last-ditch effort of the U.S. to police the Nicaraguan political system. When Washington was through with Sandino, in effect it was also through with intervention in Nicaragua, and throughout the rest of Latin America.

After his disastrous rout at Ocotal, Sandino retreated deeper into Nicaragua's interior. The mountainous terrain of the central and northern areas offered him classic geography for guerrilla actions. As described by one Marine officer at the time, these sections of Nicaragua

furnish ideal terrain for guerrilla warfare. Vast in extent, they consist of almost unbroken chains of mountains, whose rugged peaks afford ideal lookouts and whose densely forested slopes and secluded valleys furnish numerous hiding places secure from observation and attack from airplanes and inaccessible to all but the most lightly equipped of ground troops.[11]

The area is further marked by a covering of dense tropical jungle with only a few usable trails and numerous rivers passable only during the dry season (December to June). Sandino used both climate and geography to continuously escape the Marine Corps, which at the time was ill-prepared to chase the elusive guerrillas in their own backyard.

Nor was the new *Guardia Nacional* any better. From the outset, the hastily-formed *Guardia* was beset with the same kind of political problems which saw the collapse of the first one in 1926. During most of the Sandino guerrilla war, the *Guardia* was little more than an adjunct for the better-trained and equipped Marines. After the Marines began leaving, in 1929, it became the personal force of the Managua government, a role it played for the next 50 years.

Both the Marines and *Guardia* fought with the type of tactical hardships which have usually plagued conventional troops against guerrillas. They couldn't fight during the rainy season, whereas Sandino could, and did. They couldn't cross the border into Honduras, which gave Sandino an important sanctuary to hide in. As a native fighting in familiar territory, Sandino was able to develop—if necessary, by force—an elaborate network of peasant intelligence, which warned him ahead of time of Marine and *Guardia* movements.

Through persuasion, fear and coercion, Sandino was the master of the north. The politicians in the cities waited patiently for the Marines to rid the country of the festering Sandinista rebellion. After the Ocotal battle, it was thought to be only a matter of time. "It is not supposed," U.S. Minister Charles Eberhardt wrote, "that Sandino will offer much further serious resistance." At this early stage in the war, U.S. officials still underestimated Sandino and refused to think in terms of protracted guerrilla war. They would regret this later.

The Guerrilla War Begins

Immediately after the Ocotal battle, a Marine column led by Major Oliver Floyd began an intensive search to disarm the badly crippled Sandinistas. Marine intelligence had already seriously erred in its estimate of Sandino's military strength, a factor which led to the near-disaster at Ocotal. Eberhardt was reporting to Washington that, "Sandino is believed to be running low on arms . . .," but to the contrary, he was assembling a force of nearly a thousand sympathizers and obtaining arms and ammunition from friendly sources in Honduras. Although the Marines didn't know it, during the summer and fall of 1927 Sandino was in the process of organizing the population of the northern part of western Nicaragua into a complex system of intelligence and supply in preparation for the campaign ahead. This produced a deceptive lull in the fighting, which led U.S. officials to believe that Sandino was finished.

On July 29, Floyd's patrol reached Jicaro near the Honduran border but discovered that Sandino was no longer there. He was reputed to be encamped in a nearby mountain fortress known as *El Chipote*. Floyd was ordered there but by August 5 could again find nothing and gave up the search. It was like chasing a ghost. Floyd wasn't even convinced that *El Chipote* existed and ended his brief foray against Sandino believ-

28

ing his mission to be a success and that enemy forces were too badly disorganized to continue.

The Marines still didn't appreciate guerrilla war. The Brigade Commander told the American press that Sandino was "through . . . he has failed with his inferior forces." This "credibility gap" would haunt both the Coolidge and Hoover Administrations, just as it did President Johnson during Vietnam.

In September, the Sandinistas struck, out of nowhere. On the 19th, an attack was made near Telpaneca by forces under Carlos Salgado, one of Sandino's field lieutenants. It resulted in the death of two Marines and twenty-five guerrillas, and rocked the complacency of the U.S. command.

The following three months witnessed a major rise in guerrilla activity against a reduced Marine unit which, despite token reinforcements in the north, was forced onto the tactical defensive. Marine patrols which ventured deeply enough into the Segovia mountains were subjected to harassing ambushes and sniping attacks by the well-hidden enemy. The Sandinistas had no uniforms, but wore black and red kerchiefs as symbols of rebellion.

Marine aviators began reconnaissance of the north, and their efforts provided the best available intelligence on the constantly-moving Sandino. But the aviators were often fooled by Sandino's guerrilla tactics. On several occasions their bombing strategy runs hit innocent towns that the Sandinistas had evacuated. Murra and other hamlets were bombed into near ruin without any military results.

On numerous occasions these planes received ground fire from hidden bands of Sandinistas, but without losses. On October 8, their luck suddenly ran out. After a brief engagement with guerrillas, a two-seater manned by Lieutenant E. A. Thomas and Sergeant F. E. Dowdell was downed near Quilili. The two pilots were caught and macheted to death grotesquely. A photograph of Lieutenant Thomas' body hanging from a tree was found later, but a rescue patrol was ambushed near Jicaro by about 400 guerrillas and had to turn back. The bodies of the fliers were never found.

The situation in the north was fast approaching the intolerable. Marines and small *Guardia* units were holding the larger towns but numerous groups of guerrillas roamed almost at will through the country, committing murders and terrorizing the area. Although skirmishes were numerous, the Marines had been unable to successfully pursue the insurgents, mostly due to the tremendous difficulties of transportation during the rainy season and partly because of a lack of adequate forces.

Official Washington was by now more cognizant of the nature of the situation. Secretary of State Kellogg could now write that the problem in Nicaragua "is a species of guerrilla warfare which takes place in rather wild, unsettled regions of the country. . . ." The State Department, however, was still optimistic, with Kellogg expecting "that within a short time the entire burden can be assumed by the constabulary, permitting the withdrawal of the Marines." Almost the opposite, in reality, was about to happen.

The Marines and *Guardia* continued to have frequent contacts with small groups of Sandinistas, with little result, either way. In late November, however, Marine pilots finally located Sandino's headquarters on *El Chipote* Mountain. This fortress had been the subject of much earlier speculation and mystery, and some authorities had even doubted that it existed. But the Marines quickly realized the importance of the discovery. If they could corner Sandino in one place, they could get rid of him once and for all.

On December 18, Captain Richard Livingston left Matagalpa for Nueva Segovia with 6 officers and 108 men. This contingent was soon enlarged by 60 others when it was joined at Quilili by a column led by Lieutenant M. A. Richal. Both groups then began the march to wipe out Sandino's strength in the Jicaro-Chipote region. Simultaneously, small Marine units began converging northward to meet with the others near *Chipote*.

As the patrols moved, they were constantly ambushed along the route by the mobile and well-informed Sandinistas. On one occasion 200 well-armed guerrillas, some wearing Honduran Army uniforms, surprised a small Marine unit, killing one. On December 30, Sandino suddenly moved against Livingston in an apparently well-planned and concerted action. In an ambush involving about 400-500 enemy, the Marines suffered five killed and six wounded while the *Guardia* reserve lost one with two wounded. On the same day, Richal's column was attacked by about fifty Sandinistas but had only one minor casualty.

As the year 1927 closed, the Marine Command began to take serious note of Sandino's obviously improved efficiency, numbers, weapons, and discipline. They also became more suspicious that he was receiving large quantities of material aid from Honduras.

In the meantime the plodding Richal column was again ambushed, this time six miles outside of Quilali by a force of about 450. The Marines were caught in single file on a narrow trail while the insurgents struck simultaneously from several angles. The Marine first sergeant, Thomas C. Bruce, was killed, and Richal himself was wounded in the head. Superior firepower finally drove the guerrillas off but the mauled column reached Quilali on January 3, badly disorganized.

The situation was by now deteriorating rapidly. The Marines and *Guardia* sent after Sandino had not only failed to locate him but had been seriously sidetracked along the way. The U.S. *Chargé*, Dana Munro was concluding that it was "utterly impossible with the forces now available to control the whole area of Nueva Segovia," while Fleet

Admiral David Sellers noted the "fact that the bandits are apparently better organized and equipped than the Brigade Commander had reason to believe."

A Stalemate

By the beginning of the new year, it was quite apparent that the United States had not only failed to understand the Sandinista movement in a political sense but, militarily, it did not fully appreciate the terrain and weather problems as well as the nature of "small war" tactics. Sandino's power was growing despite American occupation. "They still had a lot to learn about our methods", he wrote. It would take a dramatic and substantial increase in U.S. forces to calm the country down. These began arriving in early January, 1928.

As the year turned, the situation was becoming grim. The Quilali fiasco of Livingston and Richal shook the United States out of its earlier complacency. The month of January was to witness the first in a series of Marine escalations which were to proceed throughout the year until the November election. The U.S. was now more than ever aware of the seriousness of Sandino's threat and the greatly improved capabilities of his irregular army. Sandino's enhanced position would, according to *Chargé* Munro, "make very much more difficult the destruction of his army which now seems to have been definitely undertaken."

A much stronger and determined Marine force resumed operations against the still uninvaded fortress of *El Chipote* in January. While the columns headed north, Marine air patrols scouted ahead and reported the mountain to be a beehive of guerrilla activity. On the 14th, wave after wave bombed the wooded fortress, destroying vast quantities of equipment and supplies and leaving about 45 dead. Sandino's force quickly broke up into small groups and evacuated the mountain.

By January 26, the arriving Marine ground units found the fortress empty with no trace of Sandino around. All they found were burning campfire embers and straw dummies with black and red kerchiefs (intended to draw away marine firepower.). Continued patrolling failed to come up with anything substantial, and the second mission against *El Chipote*, although it chased him away, had still not pinned Sandino down. The Sandinistas then moved southward, where they plundered ranches and small towns in the Departments of Esteli and Jinotega.

The Managua Legation then requested from the State Department permission to declare a state of war in Nueva Segovia. Washington, however, refused the request with the official rationale that such a move would convert "Sandino's status from that of a mere bandit into that of a leader of an organized rebellion, with possibilities of recognition of his belligerency by an outside power." Clearly, the State Department wished to quickly eliminate the Sandinista movement without the attendant publicity and difficulty which the term "war" would give. Never-

31

theless, the *New York Times* still noted that "not since the World War has the United States encountered such a fight as Sandino is carrying on in the mountains and jungles of Nicaragua."[12]

In a last effort to induce Sandino to surrender, Admiral Sellers penned a letter demanding his acceptance of the Stimson agreement. "It is equally superfluous," Sellers concluded, "for me to point out that the energetic and intensive campaign that our forces are shortly to inaugurate can have but one final result."

Like past efforts to cause Sandino's surrender, this too failed. The rebel leader's reply stated his immediate demands: "the only way to put an end to this struggle is the immediate withdrawal of the invading forces from our territory . . .," and, "supervising the coming elections by representatives of Latin America instead of by American Marines."

So the war went on. Sandino had been chased but not defeated. Rumors concerning his position circulated around the country but, as Admiral Sellers noted, "these reports often placed Sandino in widely separated places at the same time." Sandino was becoming a legend in his own time, and with each day that his elusive defiance went on the legend grew.

The enlarged Marine Brigade, although not positive of Sandino's exact location, kept on the offensive, pressing Sandino away from settlements. But the Marines themselves were the last to prophesy that he would soon be captured. The initial optimism of 1927 had slowly given way to a sober reality.

Sandino's tactics of attacking unexpectedly and then fleeing before the Marines could strike back, his unwillingness to give battle except in ambush, and the extreme mobility of his forces, compared to organized troops, had by early 1928 forced a reappraisal by the U.S. Command. The Commanding General was now admitting that the capture of Sandino would probably be "a matter of months or even years," while Admiral Sellers noted that the restoration of order "will be a slow process." But the country had to be pacified before the November 1928 election and, despite the new difficulties involved, Marine Commandant Lejeune expressed confidence that "we think we will be able to do it."

In early 1928, a comprehensive account of the Sandino problem as viewed by U.S. officials was cabled to Washington by General Frank R. McCoy (USA), Chief of the U.S. Electoral Mission. Its essence distills the nature of the Sandinista guerrilla war, and is worth quoting at length:

I have been seriously concerned over the military situation here. I have so expressed myself to the Marine Commandant with whom I have had daily conferences and have discussed with Admiral Sellers means for bringing about more effective prosecution of the operations. . . .

The operations are generally of a type somewhat different from those for which the normal Marine corps training and equipment are well adapted. Sandino's forces have the advantage of the local language, thorough famil-

32

iarity with the terrain, of the assistance, particularly as regards information, of elements some of which are in sympathy with Sandino while others either consider the continuance of his operations favorable to their immediate political purposes or else do not dare to incur the hostility of the outlaws by giving information or assistance to our forces. . . .

Sandino has cleverly taken advantage of the factors favoring his operations including his superior mobility. Such encounters as have occurred have been largely at times and places of his own selection and such checks as he has suffered have usually been followed by loss of contact with his forces. . . .

As regards the plan of campaign, the necessity of the elimination of Sandino by determined and unrelenting pressure and pursuit has been constantly emphasized in my interviews with General Feland. Admiral Sellers representing the Navy Department and in command of both sea and land forces is a strong man, fully conscious of his mission and of the necessity for vigorous effort.

By this stage in the campaign the military command had no illusions regarding the nature of the war they were in. A decisive defeat of the Sandinistas was no longer a practical objective. "The outlaw situation here will end," wrote General Feland, "by a collapse of their organization and a practical cessation of their activities only when their spirit is broken by constant pressure of the Marines. Such has ever been the end of Guerrilla Warfare." In early June, he realized that "to insure the early elimination of Sandino a force would be required that would be so large that it would be impossible to supply it in the country where it would have to operate." The Marines realized that they were in a war of attrition.

With the coming of the rainy season, active patrolling ended, with one exception. A river expedition of Marines was sent north in the hope that it could catch Sandino off guard, and eliminate him personally. The expedition was led by Captain Merritt A. Edson and headed north for Poteca on July 26. Although Poteca lay 400 miles upstream, Edson and his 90-man unit volunteered to make the trip up the rain-swollen Coco River in dugout canoes manned by native boatmen. As they proceeded along the hazardous river, boats capsized (intentionally, with the help of native boatmen, Edson soon realized), supplies were lost in the swift jungle river, men faltered with malaria, food ran short, and the patrol would have starved to death if it hadn't been for air drops.

But the "Coco River Patrol" forged on, undaunted. On August 7, they reached Wamblan, Sandino's main outpost in the north. The engagement which followed left one Marine and ten guerrillas dead. Following this advantage, Edson continued up the river toward Poteca, where the Sandinistas had fled. General Feland held out the hope that Edson would "virtually dispose of what is now the main body of them." Sandino's force was now in retreat with Marine planes strafing them as they moved. On August 17, the Edson column finally reached Poteca but, as had happened so often in the past, they found it abandoned.

33

Edson then sent out smaller patrols to catch the fleeing enemy but to no avail—they had already melted away into the dense countryside.

Following this chase up the river came a lull in military activity. Sandino's forces were well scattered, with roving bands moving in several directions at once. Captured prisoners told Marines that Sandino himself had crossed into Honduras. The U.S., however, was now fully committed to a fair and safe election in Nicaragua. By November, over 5,000 Marines and Bluejackets were in occupation of all major polling districts.

Meanwhile, Sandino and his lieutenants had moved back into Nueva Segovia and Jinotega. Salgado, for example, had 90 men in the Segovia mountains, but constant Marine patrolling kept him moving. The biggest objective of the Sandinistas was to disrupt the American-supervised election. With this objective in mind, Pedro Altamirano moved into Jinotega and terrorized voters against going to the polls on November 4. A Legation cable to Washington recorded his actions: "Altamirano retreated toward the border plundering inhabitants, committing various other murders [of a] wanton, brutal character. Many people [were] captured, robbed, forced to act as burden bearers, [and] otherwise mistreated." But with this last act of vengeance, Sandino's army was forced out of the populated area.

Election day was quiet. Despite Sandino's intimidation, 130,000 votes were cast, with the Liberal candidate General Moncada easily defeating his Conservative rival. Thus the Liberals obtained legally in a United States sponsored election what Washington had previously denied them in the 1926 civil war. The conclusion of the election made good part of Stimson's original agreement with General (now President) Moncada. American policy was now faced with choices for the future, particularly that part of the Agreement involving the maintenance of order. Policy had now reached a critical juncture. To a large degree, however, it was being forced by public criticism back home.

The Public Reaction

The intervention of the Coolidge Administration in Nicaragua brought forth a chorus of protest in Congress and among liberal and "anti-imperialist" segments of the general public. Mass demonstrations were held, as they were during Vietnam (but on a much smaller scale). The White House was picketed and police had to forcibly remove the protesters. The disenchantment with guerrilla warfare against the Sandinistas was an important element in evolving relations with Nicaragua.

In Congress, the political attack was led by William E. Borah (R.-Idaho), powerful Chairman of the Senate Foreign Relations Committee. He would remain the most articulate and best-known Congressional critic of the Administration's policy. During the first landings of December 1926, he proclaimed that, "the truth is, effort is being made to get this country into a shameless, cowardly little war with Mexico."[13] Other Congressional critics quickly fell in behind Borah. Early in January 1927, two resolutions were introduced in the Senate asking for a Marine withdrawal, but both were defeated.

Most Republicans in Congress remained loyal to the Administration while Democrats generally opposed the intervention. But the six-year Congressional debate over Nicaragua was not exclusively confined to party lines. Time and again prominent Republicans, in and out of Congress, rose to vigorously denounce the policies of both Coolidge and Hoover. The passion generated by the Nicaraguan debate sometimes blurred the distinction between party lines.

The situation in Nicaragua was discussed in open session in the Senate for the first time in mid-January 1927. Prominent "progressive" Republicans such as George Norris (Nebraska) and Robert La Follette (Wisconsin) hammered away at the Administration. The latter, in a fiery speech, summed up the opposition's case by pointing out that the Coolidge policy was: a) losing prestige for the U.S., b) unclear as to aims and objectives, c) intervening in a civil war, d) withholding information from the public at large, and e) waging war without Congressional consent.

These issues would remain the chief points used by Congressional critics throughout the duration of the Nicaraguan debate. With varying degrees of emphasis and intensity, spokesmen for the opposition would continually confront both Republican Presidents with similar arguments. Although the Senate and House were Republican-controlled, policy objection was so energetic and articulate that both Administrations sometimes found it necessary to pursue policies by means of Executive Agreement in order to avoid Congressional rejection. The training of the *Guardia*, supervision of Nicaraguan elections, and Marine combat against Sandino were cases in point. Like the war in Vietnam, the Sandinista war had to remain an unofficial combat.

The reports of the battle at Ocotal and the emergence of Sandino as an international figure greatly increased domestic protest. Congressional critics sharpened their attacks, and the volume of criticism during the next two years multiplied. The loss of American lives and the inability to bring the campaign to a conclusion added further fuel to the opposition fires. Senator Wheeler wondered out loud that if the Marines were engaged against "bandits," could they not be put to better use in Chicago?[14] Congressional attacks were sometimes emotional. Senator Dill, for example, labeled the intervention "one of the blackest and foulest crimes that has been committed against men."[15]

After the 1928 election in Nicaragua, pressure mounted steadily in Congress for removal of the Marines. Force reductions in 1929 and 1930 answered much of the criticism. These years saw a declining Congressional opposition, as it appeared that President Hoover, as opposed to

35

Coolidge, was moving steadily toward a withdrawal. The pace was slow, but it seemed as though the direction was correct.

The criticism of U.S. Nicaraguan policies on the part of the press and liberal groups in the nation was much less restrained than the Congressional reaction. A rash of literature from a wide variety of left-wing, "anti-imperialist" sources flooded the country. Political groups sprang up overnight to harshly condemn the United States occupation, and many of them became emotionally pro-Sandinista. Again, this was similar to Vietnam, in microcosm. Academic, clerical, labor, and other groups signed petitions demanding an immediate U.S. evacuation.

Much of the press in the United States was opposed to the Administration's policy. "The public certainly was stirred, wrote the *New York Times* correspondent, but it was stirred against the State Department. A cry arose, from many conservative newspapers as well as the liberal ones, for light on what the Administration was about in Latin America."[16]

The battle of Ocotal and its after-effects fanned into fresh flames the smoldering criticism of U.S. policy in Nicaragua. The great loss of Nicaraguan life at the hands of Marine aviation was interpreted by many policy critics as examples of American barbarism and cruelty. Even some Congressmen referred to the Marines as the country's "ambassadors of death." Atrocity stories of Marines killing and bombing innocent civilians were disseminated during the remaining years of the occupation. Horror pictures of the alleged results of Marine bombing attacks were printed.

The reports of Carlton Beals from *The Nation* probably had more influence among pro-Sandino groups than any other single source. After interviewing Sandino in Nicaragua he returned to propagate the themes of U.S. imperialism, Marine blunderings, and Sandinista patriotism. Other journals, such as *Century, Outlook*, and *Nineteenth Century*, likewise played up this theme. *The Nation* sponsored "anti-Nicaraguan" conferences.

In January 1928, a demonstration against the intervention was attended by Mrs. Franklin D. Roosevelt, William Allen White, Everett Colby, Raymond B. Fosdick, and George Foster Peabody, all powerful figures of the day. During the summer and fall of 1928, the wave of adverse criticism refused to subside, and the Caribbean policy of the United States became an issue in the presidential campaign of 1928. Prominent democrats, like Franklin D. Roosevelt, called upon the nation to renounce intervention "for all times."[17]

The Coolidge Administration's critics were certainly smaller in number than its supporters, but—as in Vietnam—the critics were much louder and more visible. Like the Congressional debate, however, dissent subsided after the Marine reductions undertaken by the Hoover Administration. Much discontent lingered on but the passion and intensity of the debate was partially undercut by the Marine withdrawals of 1929 and 1930. But the final withdrawal of all Marine units from the country in January 1933 was greeted with what one historian has called a "general rejoicing of the American press."[18]

Final Withdrawal

With the 1928 Nicaraguan elections safely behind them, U.S. authorities were no longer in a mood to continue the occupation indefinitely. "I fervently hope," wrote Assistant Secretary White, "that we will have no more elections in Latin America to supervise." Washington, however, was reluctant to withdraw all U.S. troops immediately. For one thing, Sandino's inability to interrupt the elections had produced another hope that he had given up. It will not be long now, General Feland was reporting, "until we can say that they [the guerrillas] are cleaned up." More generally, U.S. officials were fearful of the consequences of an immediate withdrawal. The State Department noted that "a withdrawal which might be interpreted as weakness could very well lead to a very disagreeable situation. . . ."

By the beginning of 1929 American policymakers had reappraised the U.S. role in Nicaragua and decided on a gradual phaseout of Marines, concurrent with a "Nicaraguanization" of the war against Sandino. During the spring and summer of 1929 over 2,000 Marines were withdrawn from Nicaragua, and by early 1930 only about 1,200 remained in the country.

This action was partly prompted by a lull in guerrilla activity. During most of 1929 Sandino was in Mexico soliciting support for his movement. In his absence his followers remained relatively quiet, a fact which prompted the Brigade Commander to comment that "this country has never been in such a peaceful state." This was the lull before the storm.

During the first months of 1930, guerrilla activity sharply increased. Sandinistas began again to raid the northern area and on several occasions were able to ambush combined Marine-*Guardia* patrols. Despite these signals of a possible return to full-scale insurgency, U.S. authorities continued reducing the Marines. The Brigade Commander was now writing pessimistically that to continue the occupation "would require many times the total available force of Marines and *Guardia*, and in addition, would produce no definite military results."

In the meantime, the Sandinistas mounted new and broader attacks. Sandino was now more aggressive, and the *Guardia*, which had taken over much of the responsibility in operations against him, was faring even worse than the Marines had before it. By late 1930 Minister Hanna was reporting that "the disorder in Nicaragua is more widespread and threatening than it has been at any time during my residence here."

37

Then, on December 31, 1930, a patrol of ten Marines left their garrison at Ocotal to repair a broken telephone line. One of Sandino's "Generals," Miguel Angel Ortez, ambushed the patrol near Achuapa, killing all but two. The remaining two, although severely wounded, managed to escape.

This massacre shattered American officials like nothing had since the Battle of Ocotal in 1927. It was also the first heavy U.S. loss in nearly two years. Minister Hanna cabled that the death of the Marines had "aroused public indignation and alarm and a greatly increased popular demand that energetic measures be adopted to terminate banditry and re-establish and restore peace in the Segovias." Nonetheless, order would have to be restored by the *Guardia Nacional*; Washington's determination to leave Nicaragua was irrevocable, despite worsening conditions.

Throughout the summer and fall of 1931, the *Guardia* continued to be plagued by Sandino's hit and run tactics. It was obvious that he was getting stronger. The *Guardia* units, even with the aid of Marine aviation, could barely keep up with him much less defeat him. The great chase was on again, but this time it was mostly Nicaraguans themselves chasing Sandino.

The only important combat activities of the Marine Corps were led by Captain Lewis B. "Chesty" Puller and his Company "M" (for mobile). Puller had great success in keeping Sandino on the run, but even his quick pursuit was unable to end the rebellion.

During the last two months of 1931 guerrilla activities more than doubled. *Chargé* Willard Beaulac wrote that, "the Nicaraguan population are generally alarmed and many fear that the movement has assumed a revolutionary character. The bandit situation appears as grave, or graver than, at any time since I have been in Nicaragua."

In early 1931, a sudden and violent earthquake had struck the capital city of Managua, destroying more than thirty full blocks. President Hoover ordered relief agencies sent down, and both Marines and *Guardia* cooperated in clearing the wreckage and providing overall assistance to the beleaguered inhabitants.

Sandino, however, interpreted this catastrophe as clearly demonstrating, in his own words, "to the doubters that divine gestures are guiding our actions in Nicaragua." While government forces were busy in Managua, his men struck swiftly and boldly on the east coast. This messianic "Robin Hood" used the earthquake disaster to his own advantage. Ironically enough, this same charge was leveled against President Somoza in 1972, when another earthquake leveled Managua. History—it seems—has a strange way of repetition.

Early in April 1931, Pedro Blandon and about 100 guerrillas looted U.S.-owned lumber and fruit concerns, and in the process mercilessly beheaded eight American employees. The town of Puerto Cabezas, sixty miles away on the Caribbean coast, was in a state of near panic. At least 400 Americans lived in this area, and demands for Marine protection flooded the Legation. But Secretary of State Stimson remained firm in his insistence upon full withdrawal, despite the earthquake. To a large degree, this was prompted by his realization that the guerrilla war was unwinnable. In his own words:

> It is now over three years since I succeeded in bringing to a conclusion the war which was going on in Nicaragua, leaving only the banditry in the northern provinces to be cleaned up . . . .

> Yet apparently we are as far from pacifying those provinces as we were three years ago. In other words, there has already been consumed a longer period of time than we required to subdue the Philippine Insurrection in 1899—a longer time than was required for the British forces to quell the guerrilla fighting in all South Africa.

Nineteen thirty-two was the worst year of the campaign. In no other year did the Sandinistas constitute such a threat to the stability of Nicaragua. Sandino's area of operations was extended to include *all* the provinces of the country except the lake region near Managua, where a skeleton Marine force was still garrisoned. The *Guardia* troops found it practically impossible to contain the guerrillas, nor could they stop the flow of supplies and the use of the Honduran border as a sanctuary.

By April 1932, Sandino appeared stronger than ever. The *Guardia* suffered a series of reverses, and on April 21, Sandino achieved his biggest military victory of the campaign near Los Puertas. He seemed on the verge of a full victory, but the Marines continued leaving on schedule.

Washington's revised estimate of Sandino was an important factor in the U.S. policy reverse. Sandino had professed all along that the major rationale for his rebellion was the presence of American forces. By the late stages of the campaign, U.S. diplomats were beginning to accept this explanation. *Chargé* Beaulac wrote Washington that the guerrilla disorders could well be "incidental to and derived from American assistance. In this connection it remains true that the avowed objective of Sandino . . . is to eject the American forces from Nicaragua." The Minister in Managua admitted that

> the possibility of conciliating Sandino will be greater if no Marines remain in Nicaragua and that even if conciliation proved to be impossible, a united Nicaragua, having deprived Sandino of his principal excuse for belligerency, that is, the presence of American Marines on foreign soil, might be in a better position to eliminate banditry than the present Government assisted by the Marines.

The Assistant Secretary himself noted that "the whole pose of Sandino . . . is that he is fighting Americans," thus a withdrawal would leave the guerrillas with "very little of a talking point left."

By late 1932, however, U.S. pessimism about the whole affair was so deep that the Assistant Secretary of State wrote that it would be "preferable to run the risk of revolutionary disturbances now and let the strong man emerge without further waste of time." Indeed, this is precisely what happened. By 1933 the U.S. was finished with intervention in Nicaragua, whatever the cost. After two decades of occupation, all the U.S. had for its efforts was more revolution in the country, domestic criticism at home, propaganda reverses internationally and a guerrilla war against peasant Sandinistas that refused to go away.

This experience remained profound in the American memory, and was a great determinant in the non-intervention policies which began with the Administration of Franklin D. Roosevelt. Ironically, Sandino himself had helped bring on the Somoza era and subsequent U.S. non-intervention policies.

But Augusto Sandino never lived to see the new era. With all the Marines gone, the *Guardia,* now led by General Anastasio Somoza, grew restless while Sandino and his followers (now up to 3000) still refused to disarm. Hostilities between the two armies flared up throughout the summer and fall of 1933. It was 1927 all over again, with civil war a *de facto* reality.

In February 1934 President Sacasa summoned both Sandino and Somoza to a peace conference in Managua. On the evening of the 21st, a dinner was held for Sandino, hosted by the President. After the festivities, Sandino and two compatriots were driven from the Presidential Palace toward downtown Managua. Crossing a *Guardia* roadblock, at ten in the evening, all three were dragged from the car, lined up and shot to death. Their bodies were quickly buried under the runway of Managua's airport.

As quickly as that, the original Sandinistas were finished in Nicaragua, Mafia-style victims of the *Guardia* and the intrigues of a political culture which knew only violence and revolution. Eight years of continuous warfare, plus over a century of revolution, had finally brought a sort of truce to the infighting of Nicaragua's tenuous political system. This truce was prompted by the emergence of Anastasio Somoza García as the chieftain of the *Guardia Nacional*, and as the main patron of U.S. interests.

V. NON-INTERVENTION AND THE SOMOZAS, 1937-1973

During the twenty-one years of occupation, the United States believed that it was acting in the best interests of both countries by promoting the twin themes of democracy and stability in Nicaragua. Washington also believed that the two were integrally related, much as they were back home in the United. States.

By 1933, conditions both inside and outside Nicaragua had forced an important change in this appraisal. For the most part, this change remained with U.S. foreign policy toward Nicaragua during the more than forty years of Somoza family rule. The contradictions and embarrassments involved in attempting to police and to democratize a foreign political system—even one as small and vulnerable as Nicaragua's—dictated this change.

The United States had learned a lesson by 1933 and, simply expressed, that lesson was this: even the greatest power, with the best of intentions, ultimately cannot force change in the basic political culture of other countries. While the United States was able to overhaul the economy, supervise elections and install presidents, the only real legacy of U.S. intervention was political stability brought about by the American-created *Guardia* and the the U.S. Marine Corps. The "strong man" was all the U.S. wanted, almost desperately, by 1933.

After twenty-one years of active occupation, the United States withdrew from Nicaragua, fully expecting the worst to happen. But the guerrilla war stopped almost as soon as the last Marine left. Washington could have let the "strong man" emerge much earlier, which would have spared the country five years of warfare. Nicaragua survived American interventionism and continued its *caudillo* politics without the Marines, and without electoral supervision from Washington. The U.S. withdrew, but the political system of Nicaragua remained behind.

41

After 1933 the United States switched diplomatic gears and pursued a non-interventionist policy toward Nicaragua. This was part of a general overhaul in U.S. Latin American policy begun under President Hoover but made famous by Roosevelt. Without attempting to condone the practices of the government in power, American foreign policy accepted, with minor deviations, the political stability which the Somoza family provided.

By and large, this was forced upon Washington by two decades of bitter experience. Nor did this imply that the U.S. was necessarily happy with the Somozas as allies. It meant simply that the U.S. finally appreciated the underlying basis of the Nicaraguan political culture, the severe limitations present for Washington to affect a lasting change, and the logic of promoting U.S. interests from a comparative distance. In short, through experience the United States matured.

The Nicaraguan political system under the Somoza family remained *in essence* what it was during the last years of American intervention. If the years of American involvement fundamentally altered the way in which Nicaraguan politicians of both parties behaved, U.S. officials were unaware of it. The United States came to realize by 1933 that it was not responsible for the *origins* of Nicaraguan political life and, try as it might, it could not be ultimately responsible for their *directions* either.

America's early contact with Nicaragua in 1912 was deceptively simple. In retrospect, this may have been responsible for later mistakes of judgment. After a few short skirmishes, the U.S. found itself in control of the whole country. Early success in directing the economy and in the installation of presidents blinded U.S. officials to the quicksand-like nature of extended political involvement

The 1926 civil war was answered by another military intervention, but this time the U.S. found itself in too deep. What appeared easy at first became almost impossible afterward, so that by 1933, earlier optimism about the wisdom of American policy had soured into abject frustration. By then, the U.S. reluctantly decided to turn inward and to abandon its original hopes for basic political change as the prerequisite for stability. In effect, practical experience and external priorities led the way, and by 1937 the Roosevelt Administration had accepted *Jefe Director* Somoza as its long-term ally.

Somoza Takes Power

The years between 1934 and 1937, however, saw Nicaragua revert to its timeless and Machiavellian pattern of "palace intrigue." With both the Sandinistas and the Marines out of the picture, a political vacuum was created. This vacuum saw two contestants vie for ultimate control of the country. President Juan Sacasa (who won the 1932 election) had titular power, but Somoza controlled the *Guardia*. Both were members

42

of the Liberal Party, and beginning in 1934, the two earnestly set out against each other in an intramural battle for Nicaragua's future.

Somoza schemed to gain the presidency through the power of the *Guardia*. Sacasa tried to stop him by holding on to the reins of the dominant Liberal Party. The closed and elitist nature of Nicaraguan politics is half-humorously seen by Somoza's attempts to take immediate power by changing his own family life.

Article 105, title 13, of the Nicaraguan Constitution prevented anyone related to the incumbent President from succeeding to the office within six months. Somoza's wife happened to be Sacasa's niece! Unwilling to wait the required six month's after Sacasa's term expired, Somoza tried to force his immediate resignation. Unable to pressure Sacasa out, Somoza then plotted to quickly divorce his own wife, Salvadorita, to end his family ties with the President! Literally, he would stop at nothing to take power.

Unsuccessful in either of these ploys, Somoza began building up support within the Nicaraguan Congress. For his part, the President countered with an attempt to create a personal *Guardia*, a sort of Nicaraguan "SS" of several hundred police. Mrs. Sacasa also got into the act. Secretly, she had gathered munitions and support from Honduras to attack Somoza's headquarters and force him out of the country. All these, too, failed, and Nicaragua's politics continued through 1935 in this form of palace intrigue version of Central American democracy.

By 1936 the Somoza-Sacasa feud was put in the open. Somoza led Managua strikers against the government and, in the process, developed a considerable following among workers. He was becoming a Nicaraguan version of Argentina's Juan Perón. He cleansed the *Guardia* of pro-Sacasa officers, and formed a private police force of his own, the *Camisas Azules* ("blueshirts"). The *Guardia*, in the meantime, branched out over the country to take control of most of the hamlets and towns. Sacasa tried to stop this activity, but it was in vain. His requests for help from Washington produced no results; the U.S. had washed its hands of Nicaraguan politics.

The end for Sacasa came with the *Guardia's* attack against the *Fortin de Acosasco*, the only remaining pro-Sacasa military post in the country. With 2,000 officers and men, Somoza assaulted the Fortin and forced its surrender on June 2, 1936. The last of President Sacasa's holdouts had gone down. The next day, the American Minister wrote: "The President is so nervous that he can't talk coherently. He insists on only one thing, getting out of the country alive." The next week he sailed to El Salvador, never again to return to Nicaragua.

With the Congress now under Somoza's domination, the *Jefe Director* spent the rest of the year ironing out the details of his coming electoral victory. Elections were postponed until December, so that there would be the legal six months gap between the resignation of the old president and the succession of the new one. The *Guardia* was placed in control of the electoral machinery, just as the Marines were in the old days.

The opposition, including Conservative ex-Presidents Chamorro and Díaz, requested U.S. supervision. When the State Department refused, they announced that they were boycotting the election. With no opposition, Somoza coasted to a landslide victory. With his inauguration on January 1, 1937 as President and *Jefe Director* of the *Guardia*, he had nearly unlimited power! The Somoza era had begun, as the notion of a nonpartisan *Guardia* vanished from sight.

Somoza's hold over Nicaraguan political life occurred because he controlled the *Guardia Nacional*. The fact that the *Guardia* was an American creation has developed the legend that Somoza's rise to power was made-in-America. The legend further grew that Somoza's domination of Nicaragua in the ensuing twenty years was also American-sponsored and endorsed.

In reality, Somoza was not an American creation, and he was never a puppet of Washington's desires. He did what most aspiring politicians in twentieth century Nicaragua did before him, namely, he used Washington as a political lever to increase and solidify his own internal ambitions.

His rise to power actually began during the formation years of the *Guardia*. His fluency in English was an important ingredient in his career. He accompanied Henry Stimson as an interpreter during the 1927 civil war, and became, thereafter, increasingly influential with U.S. authorities. The Marines knew and trusted him more than any other *Guardia* officer, and by the time of the last withdrawal in 1932 his selection as *Jefe Director* was advised by the U.S. command. President Sacasa, ironically, made the selection official and appointed Somoza as *Jefe Director* on January 1, 1933.

It was, however, Somoza's political acumen, his accessibility and ambition that promoted his rise and Sacasa's fall. He was a *caudillo* in the best Nicaraguan tradition and out-muscled and out-maneuvered his domestic foes brilliantly. He was a classic symbol of the political system from which he came. Nicaragua created Somoza, not the United States.

Born in San Marcos in the Province of Carazo on February 1, 1896, Anastasio Somoza García was brought up in a coffee-planting family with conservative traditions and wealth enough to send Anastasio, after he had received his Bachelor of Science and Arts degree at the age of eighteen from the Instituto Nacional de Oriente of Granada (Nicaragua), to Pierce Commercial College in Philadelphia.

He became a traveling auditor for the Paige Motor Company and, as one American correspondent pointed out, might have risen to the presidency of General Motors rather than that of Nicaragua had he not met and married Señorita Salvadora Debayle, daughter of one of Nicaragua's leading families, who was being schooled in the United States.

When he returned to Nicaragua, Somoza aligned himself with the Liberal Party, serving first as an interpreter. In 1925, he obtained the post of Collector of Internal Revenue for the Department of Leon. When the Liberals came to power, Somoza rose with them. He became a powerful *politico* within the party, serving as Governor of Leon and Secretary to the general commander. He was then appointed, in succession, Minister of War, Envoy Extraordinary and Minister Plenipotentiary to Costa Rica, before becoming *Guardia Jefe Director*.

Upon his inauguration in 1937, several members of the Cabinet sent in their resignations in order that he might have a free hand in forming a new ministry, and a ceremony was held in a specially constructed stand on a parade ground, attended by a large crowd. In his inaugural address, Somoza aped Franklin D. Roosevelt, a style which he perfected to a high art in the years ahead. He promised a Nicaraguan "New Deal" which included development of the gold industry, canalization of the San Juan River, harnessing of hydroelectric power and completion of Nicaragua's section of the Pan American Highway.

His "friendship" with the United States, however, was his own creation, not Roosevelt's. It happened to serve the interests of both countries for the promotion of stability in the dangerous late 1930's. Somoza cleverly used Washington's non-interventionist policies to his own advantage. This did not prevent him, however, from pursuing his own objectives. In 1938, for example, a border war with Honduras seemed imminent. When the U.S. refused arms to Nicaragua, Somoza went elsewhere and bought them from the Axis.

The next year he was rewarded for this balancing act with an official invitation to visit Washington, an event which became the highlight of his career. With Roosevelt, meeting him personally at the train station, Somoza got the red carpet. He milked cows at Purdue, attended state fairs, and baseball games and, in a dinner held in his honor, made the following toast to President Roosevelt:

If the United States should ever get into a war, which is against our hopes, Nicaragua will put 10,000 well-trained men at the service of the United States within twenty-four hours. There will be forty thousand within sixty days, besides our landing fields and other facilities.

To the *Christian Science Monitor* correspondent, Somoza remarked:

I am personally friendly with the United States. As Chief Executive of my nation I also must remain friendly with the United States—as long as the United States is strong.[19]

"Somoza might be a son-of-a-bitch," Cordell Hull is said to have quipped, but "he's our son-of-a-bitch."

The First Somoza Government

Inside Nicaragua, Somoza's power and wealth grew immeasurably. Nicaragua became, in effect, his personal *hacienda*. The functions of the *Guardia* were greatly expanded to include internal revenue, transportation, postal services and sanitation. It was the country's only police force and army combined. Nobody could leave the country or start a business without *Guardia* permission. As *Jefe Director*, Somoza became, in fact, *caudillo* in the grand Nicaraguan tradition. He also grew extremely wealthy.

In control of the administrative apparatus of the country, President Somoza soon became a powerful landowner and entrepreneur in his own right. At less than cost, he bought the best land available. He used the country's public works budget to build up his own property, with the *Guardia* often providing free labor. He planted coffee farms and developed a cattle empire.

By the end of World War II he became the richest person in the history of Nicaragua. He owned 48 houses, 51 ranches, 46 coffee plantations, 18 farms, 8 sugar plantations and mills, 18 industrial plants, 76 urban and 16 rural unimproved properties. The trucks used on his private ranches and the gasoline to run them were supplied by the *Guardia*. Most of his farmhands were listed as soldiers and paid by funds from the national budget.

His salary as a government official provided him with pocketmoney. In addition, foreign mining companies operating in Nicaragua paid him $3,000 per month to authorize the export of precious metals; he received fifteen percent of the entire production of the Las Segovias gold mine, estimated at ten million dollars annually; he was the principal stockholder in the National Brewery.

The life of a *caudillo*, however, was not carefree. During Somoza's regime the Presidential Palace at Managua resembled a beleaguered fortress. Detachments of the National Guard constantly patrolled the grounds. On each side of the door to the President's office stood a machine gun, loaded and ready for action, attended by a squad of *Guardia*. When he drove through the city in a large closed Cadillac, upholstered in red and beige and protected by a bulletproof body and glass, the car was surrounded by armed guards.

But Somoza ruled by more than just money and force. The charisma which helped carry him to power also helped maintain him there. An anecdote provided by the American journalist John Gunther in 1940 explains the personal qualities which helped make Anastasio Somoza President Roosevelts' ally and Nicaragua's ruler for twenty years:

President Somoza is the absolute and undisputed boss of Nicaragua, but he enjoys informality. He is a cheerful host. He seats his guests in rocking chairs, gives them cooling refreshment, and talks—in as good American English as can be imagined—a steady, persuasive, bubbling stream. He likes to call the American minister "Boy." Once Mrs. Meridith Nicholson, the minister's wife, complained mildly that there was no good milk in Managua. The next day she found a first-class cow on her doorstep, the gift of the President.[20]

The personal side of the Somoza era, however, became a scandal. From the beginning of his regime, all government posts were filled with personal friends, favorites and members of his numerous family. He would appoint unknown persons to government positions on impulse and then, later, remove them for the same reason. Both of his sons, Luis and Anastasio Debayle, were sent to the United States for schooling, and for grooming as potential *caudillos* in their own right (which, in fact, they both became). His son-in-law, Guillermo Sevilla Sacasa, was made Ambassador to the United States, a post he held until Anastasio II was deposed in 1979.

The ceremony making Somoza's daughter, Lillian, "Queen of the Army" is a case study of the Hollywood-like nature of the Nicaraguan fiefdom he ruled. After attending finishing school in Washington she was called back to Managua for the bestowed honor, one which contained all the elements of a Chaplin comedy. The day of the great event was proclaimed a national holiday. Lillian slowly drove through the streets of the capital in a gilt chariot, escorted by officers of the Nicaraguan armed forces decked out in Roman togas. Behind the triumphal chariot marched employees of various government departments, her "obedient servants." The royal procession wound its way to the Cathedral, where the Archbishop of Managua placed upon the Queen's brow a gold crown, and in her hands a jeweled scepter.

Beneath the comic-opera surface, however, lay a profound seriousness. Somoza had no intention to let another *caudillo*, Liberal, Conservative or Sandinista, take his place. The last Sandinista holdout was Pedro Altamirano, who emerged in 1937 by sacking coffee plantations and small towns near the Coco River. This "ghost" of Sandino was quickly liquidated by the *Guardia Nacional*, who caught him asleep in his headquarters one night and cut off his head with a machete. By bringing the head back to Managua for public display, Somoza ended the years of unofficial warfare between the *Guardia* and the Sandinistas.

In 1939 Somoza used a pliant Nicaraguan Congress to extend his presidency for nine years, without elections. He used the *Guardia* to end dissent from the Conservative Party when his troops raided Conservative headquarters and arrested fifty-six of their leaders. Although they were all released within a day, the point was made.

Somoza also tried to make the *Guardia* a true military force. He reopened the *Academia Militar* and negotiated with the U.S. for American instructors. Anastasio II was sent to West Point. Upon his graduation in 1946, he was appointed Commander of the First Battalion at La Loma. A Nicaraguan Air Force (FAN) was begun with the purchase of

47

aircraft from the U.S. under a Lend Lease agreement. By the end of World War II, the FAN had nearly 40 planes. An infant Nicaraguan Navy was also started with Somoza's purchase of patrol boats and a U.S. Coast Guard cutter for $1500.

Somoza was careful to cultivate the impression of strong U.S. backing for his regime, more of a fiction than a reality. His sense of theater showed a brilliant political imagination, one any U.S. politician would envy. When FDR won a landslide victory in 1940, Somoza called a two-day national holiday. In 1942 he honored Roosevelt's birthday by renaming Managua's main street "Avenida Roosevelt." He was a master politician, but opposition from within the country surfaced early, as it nearly always did in Nicaragua's stormy history.

In 1944, when his term still had three years to run, the question of a successor began to plague the *politicos* of the Liberal Party. Attempts to draw Somoza out on the subject met with stony silence.

Finally, a group of party leaders called upon him to ask for some clarification. The president heard them out, then glanced at them sarcastically. "And whom do you propose to elect in my place?" he asked. Several names were mentioned; at each Somoza refused comment. Finally, he spoke: "Perhaps you are thinking of electing Arguello." He laughed loudly and contemptuously. Leonardo Arguello was a 73-year-old physician and literary pretender. An old party wheel horse, without personality or prestige, he was serving as Somoza's Minister of Interior. If Somoza could not run himself, Arguello might serve as his "Trojan Horse."

Somoza's hold over Nicaraguan politics obviously depended on much more than mere force! Nobody could survive in such a chaotic atmosphere without a masterful sense of political savvy. Somoza was head-and-shoulders above them all. As a political tactician, he was at times brilliant. By 1944 the country was growing restless under his domination. Agitators among university students, the Conservative Party, underground labor groups (unions had been banned) and agents from other Central American countries embarked upon a full-scale offensive against his regime. Demonstrations and riots flared up and calls were issued for a general strike. Somoza closed the universities and arrested scores of workers and students. The strike never materialized.

In an intuitive counterstrike, Somoza then reversed course. Pulling the rug out from under the opposition, he patronizingly vetoed a measure of Congress which would have allowed his re-election in 1947. Emulating Argentina's Juan Perón, he then suddenly passed ultra-liberal labor laws. By any standards, particularly Central American, these were extremely progressive. Going even further, Somoza released political detainees; he authorized anti-government rallies and permitted open criticism of him by the opposition press. While the *Guardia* remained in its barracks, an anti-Somoza parade of 100,000 marched on

Managua. In January 1946, Somoza publicly announced that he would not run for the presidency the next year.

The 1947 election was marked by controversy and confusion. Towards nightfall on election day, with results uncertain, the *Guardia* abruptly closed the polls and rushed the ballots away. The next day, Somoza announced that his candidate, Dr. Arguello, had won. The opposition charged fraud and intimidation and even flew to Washington to present their case. Nothing was proved, and the U.S. granted recognition to the new government. Arguello was inaugurated on May 1, 1947, but he didn't last long.

His inauguration speech was a shock to all Nicaragua, especially General Somoza. With an ambition no one had ever expected from him, the new President declared: "You may be certain that I shall not be simply a decorative figure in this high office."

His first actions gave proof to his words. He removed the Chief of Police of Managua, an ardent Somoza supporter, and revoked all appointments to federal office made by Somoza during his term. He appeared in public without a bodyguard and developed a following among the population. Drunk with this sudden popularity, Arguello decided on a new and more dangerous step: he ordered the transfer of Major Anastasio Somoza Debayle to an inferior post in the Department of Leon. Touching Somoza's own family, this was going too far.

Twenty-five days after his inauguration, Arguello's time was up. At 2:00 A.M. on May 26, the *Guardia* seized the National Palace and the Managua police barracks. Arguello's telephone lines were cut, and officers loyal to him were dragged from bed and placed under arrest. Congress was surrounded and ordered to handpick Dr. Benjamin Sacasa—another Somoza protege—as the new President. Arguello sought asylum in Mexico, after one of the shortest presidencies in history, remarkably brief even by Nicaraguan standards.

When Somoza needed guile, he used it imaginatively. When he needed force he did the same, without shedding a drop of blood. The 1947 coup, however, temporarily ended any pretensions of friendship with the United States. The Truman Administration refused recognition, recalled all U.S. military personnel in Nicaragua and froze the aid program. Nicaragua's perennial revolutionary, the Conservative Emiliano Chamorro, tried a counter-coup but was sent fleeing to Mexico under air attacks from the FAN. Hundreds of opposition leaders were arrested. As *Jefe Director* of the *Guardia,* and with a new handpicked president, Somoza presided over a Nicaragua that was quiet but unrecognized.

U.S. nonrecognition of Nicaragua didn't last very long either. In conformity with a 1948 OAS resolution for continuity of recognition among Latin American states, the U.S. granted recognition back to Nicaragua. The new regime, under General Somoza's tutelage, moved again toward a "liberalization" process. Chamorro was allowed to return from Mexico under a compromise political arrangement giving the Conservatives various government posts and at least one-third of Congressional seats. In the 1950 election between Somoza (chosen, of course, by the Liberals) and Chamorro, Somoza won re-election by over 100,000 votes.

Undaunted, the Conservative leader Chamorro tried another coup in 1954. A group of conspirators led by him and aided by the Costa Rican government planned to assassinate Somoza in an ambush. The plot failed miserably. Somoza then took much of his vengeance against President José Figueres of Costa Rica, his most dangerous enemy in Central America.

Nicaraguan relations with Costa Rica had been strained for many years. The element of regional relations in Central America tells much of the story of the internal politics of Somoza's presidency, and would continue to be a thorn in the side of his successors. Somoza's domestic opponents were openly aided by his foreign enemies, and Costa Rica was, in his mind, the chief offender. Somoza had tried, in 1948, to crush the Figueres government by force, but was beaten back.

After the 1954 attempt against him by President Figueres, Somoza purchased 25 P-51 aircraft from Sweden, which made the FAN Central America's largest Air Force. A Somoza-backed force of disguised *Guardia* and Costa Rican exiles tried in 1955 to remove Figueres. This also failed, and Central America's "Cold War" continued, between intermittent and bizarre episodes of mini-invasions, coups and failed plots.

The global Cold War also shaped Somoza's foreign policy. He became a hard-line foe of world communism and used this point brilliantly to attract U.S. aid. There was no stronger anti-communist government in the world than Nicaragua's. When the U.S. turned against the Guatemalan Communist regime of Jacob Arbenz in 1954, Somoza offered Nicaraguan soil as a strategic base. Large amounts of U.S. arms and munitions landed in Nicaragua, and hundreds of Somoza's *Guardia* crossed the border with Guatemalan exiles in the final assault against Arbenz.

In the last few years of his presidency, aside from his problems with Costa Rica, Somoza's rule had settled into a form of normalcy. True, there were the chronic revolutionary tries by Chamorro and his supporters, but they never got anywhere. The economy was going through a fairly prosperous time, Somoza's leadership was firm and undisputed, U.S. aid was coming in and his ties with Washington were cemented by his strong friendship with U.S. Ambassador Thomas Whelan.

This bubble burst, however, on September 20, 1956 when a radical poet from Leon pumped four shots at point-blank range into his body. Seconds later, the *Guardia* riddled the assassin, Rigoberto Perez, with rifle shells, but it was too late. Their General and Nicaragua's political boss for twenty years, died three days later. The first Somoza era had ended, but a new one was about to begin.

Second & Third Somozas

The late president had provided well for his succession. His son Luis had already been made President of the Congress and was selected as First Designate for the presidency. Anastasio II was Acting *Jefe Director* of the *Guardia* when his father died and was also Commander of the Air Force.

The major threat to the sons came from the Minister of War, Colonel Francisco Gaitán, a twenty-year veteran of the *Guardia* with great power among the ranks. Gaitán was quickly dispatched as Ambassador to Argentina, with orders never to come back. These he carried out for ten years, until he returned to Nicaragua shortly before his death.

As *Jefe Director,* Anastasio II arrested much of the opposition, including Emiliano Chamorro's nephew, Pedro Joaquín Chamorro, editor of *La Prensa,* the chief opposition paper to the government. Chamorro, as usual, was released shortly afterward. But with Luis Somoza as the Liberal candidate, and Anastasio as *Guardia* Director, the Conservatives boycotted the election, just as they did in 1936. The results were overwhelmingly for Luis Somoza.

Luis' government was reminiscent of the way his father governed when the opposition was quiet. Most American critics of the Somozas forget this, but it is nearly impossible to rule "democratically" under a never-ending threat of revolution or civil war. As President, Luis Somoza, however, became a fairly reformist *caudillo*. He made overall important political changes, including a constitutional resurrection of the clause prohibiting succession to the presidency of any relative of the incumbent. He announced that he would serve only one term, a promise he kept faithfully. The internal role of the *Guardia* was downplayed, and the military budget was reduced by $1.5 million. Although during most of his presidency the country was under martial law, freedom of the press was greatly expanded.

This encouraged Pedro Joaquín Chamorro, fourth generation of the revolutionary Conservative family, to try still another armed coup. An attack from Costa Rica, led by him, was defeated in 1959. He and his supporters were back in prison, but came out again the next year. In-again, out-again was becoming the opposition's lot in the hectic political atmosphere of the Somozas' Nicaragua.

During Luis Somoza's years, the Nicaraguan economy boomed. Cotton, textiles and other manufactures provided a high employment. The middle class grew faster, and the economy begat a "white collar" set of entrepreneurs for the first time. American loans rose dramatically and Nicaragua—including the Somoza family—profited. The foreign policy ties with Washington grew even stronger, especially in light of the Castro regime in Cuba.

With the coming to power of a Communist beachhead in the region, the opposition in Nicaragua grew bolder. Beginning in 1960, armed excursions against Somoza—most of a minor nature—became commonplace, with many using Costa Rica as a launching base.

But Nicaragua and the U.S. grew closer. When President Kennedy formed the abortive Bay of Pigs invasion against Cuba in 1961, he used Nicaragua as a base for most of the ground and air attacks.

When Luis stepped down from the presidency in 1963, his hand-picked successor was René Shick. The Conservatives had their own candidate, but his lack of ability, plus voter apathy, made them boycott the election again. Shick's government continued in the manner of Luis Somoza, and even succeeded in limiting some of the power and prestige of the *Guardia*. The most important event of the era, however, was the foundation of a Marxist and Cuban-inspired version of second-generation Sandinistas, the Sandinista National Liberation Front (FSLN).

Formed in Cuba in 1961 by Carlos Fonseca Amador, this small group of radical youth began training to overthrow the government by the Fidel-Che tactic of guerrilla warfare. Fonseca and his chief collaborator, Tomás Borge Martinez, underwent extensive indoctrination and military training in Cuba before departing for Nicaragua in 1963.

About 60 of them set up a base in Matagalpa in the northern mountains and tried, unsuccessfully, to rally native peasants to their cause. During the remainder of the decade they would sporadically raid mining camps and outpost towns, with little concrete results. In 1964 Fonseca was found by the government and arrested. President Shick's intervention, however, had him exiled rather than imprisoned. In 1967, the FSLN was forced further underground after being routed in pitched battle with the *Guardia*.

President Shick died in office in 1966, replaced by Minister of Interior Lorenzo Guerrero, a close Somoza protege. The following year Luis Somoza also died, leaving only one obvious candidate for the presidency.

During the Shick years, Anastasio Somoza II had retained his post as *Jefe Director* of the *Guardia*. Under his guidance, the *Guardia,* bolstered by U.S. aid and counterinsurgency training, grew more powerful. Jet fighters from Washington strengthened the FAN, keeping it the best Air Force in Central America. Officers loyal to Somoza were kept and promoted, others were not. He would need a strong and loyal force, because the 1967 election was to prove one of the most violent in Nicaraguan history.

In addition to a beefed-up and confident *Guardia,* Somoza also formed a modern version of his father's "blueshirts", AMOROCS (Asociación Militar de Oficiales Retirados Obreros y Campesinos Somocistas). Both groups openly intimidated the opposition, which by now had collaborated in a coalition of parties called the National Opposition Union (UNO).

Pedro Joaquín Chamorro then used his own violence to try another attempt at revolution. Bringing over 40,000 opposition supporters into Managua on January 22, many of them armed, he called for a *Guardia* revolt against Somoza. When the crowd tried to march on the presidential palace, the *Guardia* opened fire, killing 40 and wounding over 100 more. Somoza ended the rebellion with tanks, while Chamorro and 600 followers escaped into the *Gran Hotel*. Here, they held tourists as hostages until mediation from the U.S. Embassy and the Catholic Church secured their safe release. In this atmosphere, Anastasio Somoza II was elected president in a landslide, the third Somoza to receive such a "mandate."

After his arrest, Chamorro was placed in prison, but *La Prensa* still continued its open attacks on the government. The economy continued to expand, and per capital income rose from $331 to $685 between 1967 and 1976. Housing units increased, as did education. The GNP went up 8 percent, and manufacturing grew by 10 percent, the second largest rate in Latin America (to Brazil).

Somoza's personal fortune also soared. Different sources placed it between $50 and $300 million. His landholdings were over a third of all the country's registered property. He owned vast farms of cotton, sugar, coffee and beef—the nation's main exports, plus smaller holdings of cocoa, tobacco and produce. His family owned the shipping line, the airline, the cement plant, textile and sugar mills. In his father's footsteps, Anastasio II was becoming one of Latin America's richest men.

In the meantime, the FSLN—having failed in the mountains—tried the tactic of urban guerrilla warfare. Here they were no more successful than before. After a series of daring bank hold-ups, the *Guardia* crushed the Managua FSLN in 1969. They then moved to Costa Rica, where Carlos Fonseca Amador was promptly imprisoned for bank robbery. The Costa Rican authorities kept him locked up until his FSLN followers hijacked a Costa Rican airliner. The plane was returned only after Fonseca and three others were released from jail and flown to Cuba.

The new Sandinistas were receiving international attention, just like their forebear, with two main differences: they now had the active support of a regional power (Cuba) plus the ideological and material backing of a powerful and energetic communist movement which they fully accepted. Augusto Sandino had neither.

Inside Nicaragua, Somoza's power base began a slow erosion. A radicalized Catholic Church, led by the Marxist post-priest Ernesto Cardenal, began overt criticism of the regime. Scandals in the *Guardia* lowered its prestige, including that of its *Jefe Director*. The public murder of another *Guardia* officer by Major Oscar Morales revealed disunion in its ranks to the whole nation. The growing white collar and middle-class began to resent the President's financial power. Like his father, however, Somoza still had a political ace up his sleeve.

Fresh from a trip to the United States, where he received the blessings of President Nixon, Somoza came back to Nicaragua with renewed vigor. In March, 1971 he concluded a political truce with the UNO coalition. This arrangement called for the dissolution of Congress, the creation of a constituent assembly, and the appointment of a three-man *junta* (including Somoza) to govern until elections in 1974. Somoza, of course, remained *Guardia Jefe Director*.

This truce might have worked better in practice than it actually did, were not for the intervention—this time—of natural causes. A devastating earthquake hit Managua on December 23, 1972—the same type of quake which occurred back in 1931. Most of the city was reduced to rubble, 10,000 were killed, hundreds of thousands left homeless and over 75 percent of commercial enterprises destroyed. The occasion was tragic and opened the way for anarchy and violence.

Massive looting left the capitol almost out of control. With elements of the *Guardia* participating in the looting, the force sunk to a new low in public esteem. Charges of corruption and graft were leveled against the government, and the historic "social contract" between business and the government grew fragile. There were rumblings in the air.

With the close support of U.S. Ambassador Turner Shelton, however, Somoza clamped down on the political opposition and looked to Washington for disaster relief. The 1971 truce was abandoned; the president now ruled by decree. Massive public and private aid helped see the country through the period of turmoil. Most of the aid, however, went through Somoza's banks, to be funneled through Somoza's construction companies and cement and roofing companies.

Squeezed by such profiteering, the middle-class became more alienated. Downtown Managua, meanwhile, was sealed off by barbed wire, and hundreds of thousands of people were evacuated elsewhere. Gradually, the country began to get back on its feet.

In retrospect, however, the Somoza government never fully recovered its confidence and power after the earthquake. This disaster did more than destroy a city; its ultimate effects helped topple the last of the trio of Somoza rulers. It was an event of profound human and political importance. Fairly or not, Somoza, his government and the *Guardia*, were increasingly tarred with the brush of public scandal, profiteering and corruption.[21] Internal opposition grew clandestinely and in stages. The Catholic Church turned almost officially against him, and the middle class grew more and more alienated. The new Sandinistas grew bolder and renewed their guerrilla warfare in the rural hills.

54

As the years after the earthquake went by, Somoza's actions appeared more bizarre and quixotic; he seemed to be losing his hold over the country. Appearances can be as important as reality. After the earthquake, Nicaragua *appeared* to be heading downhill. With the government pushed onto the political defensive, Cuban and other communist scavengers saw their chance. Aided by Somoza-haters in the United States, a full-scale international offensive against him began in 1974. This was the beginning of the end.

VI. REVOLUTION AND THE NEW SANDINISTAS: 1974-1982

In retrospect, the decades of U.S. non-intervention after 1933 were more of a legal fiction than a political reality. Intervention is a relative and flexible term. The United States, to be sure, had no military forces in Nicaragua. It did not dictate the economy nor did it supervise elections. Nicaragua was left on its own course, and Washington, for the most part, let events control themselves. But U.S. power was so overwhelming, even in its absence, that the hovering shadow of Washington continually helped shape the direction of things, if only from a distance.

U.S. intrusion was important, but not decisive. During the 1940's, for example, State Department influence was instrumental in persuading Somoza I against running for re-election, but Washington's non-recognition of his 1947 coup failed to remove him. In the 1950's, the anti-communist policies of the Eisenhower Administration forged an alliance of both convenience and necessity for Nicaragua. American aid, which increased in the 1960's, was a strong and visible show of support for both Luis and Anastasio II. Strictly speaking, this was not intervention in the earlier sense, but Washington's assistance and overt cooperation with the government were universally acknowledged as a form of at least tacit approval.

Intervention has two sides, negative and positive. Given the enormous power and prestige of the United States in Latin America, both sides are important. At any point during the last four decades, a strong and consistently negative U.S. policy toward Nicaragua could have toppled any of the Somozas. At the very least, the U.S. could have isolated them economically and politically. Their rule would have been nearly unmanageable.

But the U.S., for strategic and historic reasons, never went that far. Nicaragua was an ally and was treated as such. In turn, the Somozas used the U.S. in the same manner. It was a marriage of convenience

57

and interest. "Friendship" between countries is a utopian's dream, a smokescreen which masks underlying strategic and political interests.

By the mid-1970's the alliance between Nicaragua and the United States was beginning to loosen. Ater the 1972 earthquake, it was apparent that the Nicaraguan government had real problems. The fall of President Nixon after Watergate set Somoza's international prestige back considerably. Nixon had been a valuable symbol of the alliance with the United States.

It was in 1974 that the Somoza regime began its historic downslide inside Nicaragua. By 1978 a hostile Carter Administration plus an international media and military offensive pushed the Nicaraguan government even further against the wall. The end was nearing.

The Countdown on Somoza

The 1974 elections became a boring repetition of previous disputes. For the fifth time since 1936 the Conservatives (and the opposition coalition) found it necessary to boycott the obvious results. Pedro Joaquín Chamorro, as usual, led the opposition's dissent, while the Archbishop of Managua announced from the pulpit that he was not even going to vote. Somoza, as if on cue, announced the suspension of Chamorro's political rights.

The September election produced the usual Somoza victory. The United States, now under President Gerald Ford, then recalled Somoza's closest U.S. collaborator, Ambassador Turner Shelton.

Dismayed, but not undaunted, President Somoza held a series of elaborate gatherings for Shelton. The last one was on December 27, 1974, a date which marks the unofficial beginning of the new Sandinista guerrilla offensive.

Shortly after ten o'clock at night, an assault group of FSLN guerrillas burst into the party, being hosted by former Agriculture Minister José María Castillo. Guns blazing, they killed two *Guardia* soldiers and a private bodyguard. Although their prize object—Ambassador Shelton—had already left, the Sandinistas had a remarkable catch. They captured several prominent Somoza politicians, including the Foreign Minister, the Mayor of Managua, and Nicaragua's Ambassador to the United States (Somoza's son-in-law).

President Somoza was out of Managua when the attack occurred, but he hurriedly rushed back to the scene. Persuaded from storming the house frontally, Somoza bitterly agreed to allow the guerrillas safe passage to Cuba and a ransom of $1 million in exchange for the hostages.

The Sandinistas, thus, burst upon the worldwide terrorist and kidnapping scene with their own homegrown "hostage crisis." In one bold sweep, they succeeded in bringing international humiliation to the government and in giving their own cause a powerful boost. But it was the Nicaraguan people who would have to pay the price, both for the

FSLN's fanatical violence and for the government's own responses. Nicaragua was again at war with itself.

Somoza immediately declared a state of seige throughout the country, one which would last for 33 months. Constitutional guarantees were suspended, the press was strictly censored, and a special military tribunal was set up to investigate the FSLN. An 80 percent increase in U.S. military aid was obtained from the Ford Administration, and an elite 800-man counterinsurgency force was sent into the Department of Matagalpa against Sandinista hideouts. Resettlement camps were formed for the parts of the population that were uprooted. The area became a fire-free zone, in a Nicaraguan version of "strategic hamlet" counterguerrilla warfare tactics.

The *Guardia* was able to quiet the country down, at least for the time being. The *Frente's* founder, Carlos Fonseca Amador, was killed in action in late 1976. The guerrilla movement appeared over.

But those Americans who remembered the Marine Corps' struggles against Augusto Sandino a generation ago would know that a lull in guerrilla war can be extremely deceptive. Although militarily successful in the short-run, the *Guardia* was not able to eliminate the Sandinistas entirely, nor could it close the growing chasm between Somoza, the Church and the middle class.

In 1977 the Somoza government also began to run head-on against a mounting chorus of criticism, both domestic and international. The *Guardia* was accused of systematic repression against the rural population. In a pastoral letter from Nicaragua's Catholic Archbishop, the *Guardia* was charged with "humiliating and inhuman treatment ranging from torture and rape to summary execution." Left-wing and liberal groups outside of Nicaragua, such as Amnesty International, publicly accused Somoza of widespread "human rights" abuses.

The American columnist, Jack Anderson, went after Somoza in print with a rare degree of personal vendetta. Anderson's columns had great influence and popularity, and his readers were given a grotesque portrait of Somoza's personal life as the "world's greediest ruler." Alan Riding of the *New York Times* was also widely-read and equally anti-Somoza, but with less emotion than Anderson.

On the other hand, the American media remained silent—or strangely ignorant—on the documented cases of Sandinista brutality and violence. The information "war" in the world's press was clearly one-sided against the Somoza government.

Amidst the mounting media campaign against him, President Somoza's personal life also deteriorated. This did his international standing much harm, and gave further evidence of his government's gradual decline. His U.S.-born wife no longer even appeared in public with him, replaced by his mistress, "Dinora." He had public problems with both daughters; one fled to London after an alleged romance with an FSLN member was broken up. His son Anastasio, the next in line as *Jefe Director*, was dismissed from Sandhurst. Other family members were touched with various private scandals. Somoza's health declined and he gained considerable weight. In 1977 he suffered a serious heart attack and had to be flown to Miami for treatment. But like the proverbial sea captain, Somoza went back to stay with his "ship" to the end.

The end for Somoza came from a combination of three sources: the growing alienation against him inside the country, the international support given to the FSLN, and the adversarial posture of the Carter Administration. By mid-1979, the new Sandinistas had taken advantage of all three and found themselves in control of the country. In 1977, this appeared almost impossible.

Strategic cooperation with the Somoza government (with temporary exceptions) had been a fundamental pillar of U.S. foreign policy for over forty years. When the Carter Administration came to Washington in 1977, however, this policy underwent a subtle but significant reverse.

Policy-makers who reflected the strategic and national interest tradition were replaced by a new breed of human rights activists. By mid-1977 most of the Ford Administration personnel were gone. The loss of these experienced political realists, such as Ambassador James D. Theberge, opened a brief but radical new era in U.S. foreign policy. The American new left was about to confront Nicaragua's old guard.

Pressure on the executive branch to withdraw support from "authoritarian" governments in Latin America had been building in the U.S. Congress since at least 1974. The military overthrow of Chile's President Salvador Allende resulted in a series of Congressional investigations into the role of the CIA in clandestine operations in Chile. In 1975, Congress passed the Harkin Amendment, prohibiting assistance to countries that violated the human rights of their own citizens. Chile, Uruguay and Argentina were first on the list. With the Carter Administration's emphasis on human rights diplomacy, Somoza's Nicaragua became the new American target.

In April 1977 the Carter Administration began to take action on human rights grounds to delay certain military sales items. Still, the military and economic assistance program continued until 1979. Under President Carter, Nicaragua became a near-perfect showcase for human rights moralism. Guatemala, Honduras and El Salvador were also included as "violators," in a hemisphere-wide offensive against conservative governments. The Administration's Assistant Secretary of State for Human Rights, Patricia Derian, travelled through Latin America in a much-public display of concern and investigation over alleged abuses, country by country. But events in Nicaragua were moving even faster than Miss Derian.

In late 1977 the supposedly contained Sandinistas launched a concerted series of ambushes against the *Guardia* in five Nicaraguan towns.

The FSLN was forced back into the mountains by superior firepower, but the attacks caught the government off balance again. Memories of 1974 were coming back.

In a rare display of middle class defiance, twelve prominent Nicaraguans, including a Maryknoll priest, Miguel d'Escoto, met in Guatemala and signed a joint statement demanding that the FSLN be invited to participate in the government. Somoza was being slowly strangled by his friends, his allies and his enemies—a deadly combination.

He was also his own worst enemy, in several respects. Somoza might have retained the allegiance of the Nicaraguan population if he had taken certain steps to shore up his beleaguered regime. But he did very little. He could have clamped down on corruption inside the government. He could have announced more reforms in the social areas. He could have placated the growing upper and middle class resentment against his wealth. He could have also held strong against the first Sandinista hostage crisis of December 1974, which would have forced the terrorists into the notoriety of either backing down or killing the hostages.

For its part, the U.S. government failed to promote the transfer of power inside Nicaragua to a government not dominated by the Sandinistas. According to the Nicaraguan Constitution, no member of the Somoza family was eligible to succeed to the presidency in the elections scheduled for 1981. But the U.S. was so obsessed with uncovering the human rights sins of the Somoza government that it failed to help plan a constitutional succession to his regime. Instead of reaching out constructively to promote a viable alternative and a constitutional solution, the U.S. remained a relatively helpless and negative bystander until it became too late.

The Last Year

The year 1978 was the last full year of Somoza power in Nicaragua. It opened inauspiciously for the President. On January 10, a gang of thugs assassinated Somoza's perennial political opponent, *La Prensa* editor Pedro Joaquín Chamorro. The nation erupted in a spasm of outrage and violence. Crowds were in the streets, night and day, for two weeks. A general strike called by business leaders was 90 percent effective. Somoza's resignation was demanded, as there was a widespread suspicion—never proven—that Somoza was somehow responsible for Chamorro's death.[22]

For the next six months the country was plagued by continuous, sporadic violence, most of it uncoordinated. In the February elections, 52 candidates formally dropped out. Only one-third of the voters bothered to show up at the polling houses.

Somoza's public appearances were made behind a screen of bulletproof glass. In an attempt to emulate what his father did in similar

61

circumstances in the 1940's, he announced a package of labor reforms to the public. But this time it didn't work. The country never returned to normal.

A full-scale rebellion was now underway. First the construction workers struck, then the municipal and hospital workers. All over the country, the universities were empty. Riots flared.

The Sandinistas took full advantage of the prevailing anarchy by recruiting legions of radical youth to their ranks. They spent months gathering and organizing their forces in both the rural and urban areas. They stockpiled arms, which were now being generously smuggled in from a variety of international centers.

Indeed, from the very beginnings in Cuba in 1961, the new Sandinistas were backed by an international network of terrorists, revolutionaries and Cuban-inspired communists. During its formative years, Cuba was homebase for hundreds of FSLN trainees. Scores of pro-Sandinista "political action" groups appeared in the U.S. and throughout Latin America. Prominent Catholic priests, especially from the Maryknoll Society, backed the FSLN cause. This civil war was also an international one.

The Sandinistas also received direct and indirect assistance from other Latin American governments. Some, like Costa Rica, had a long score to settle with the Somozas. Hundreds of FSLN combat soldiers from Panama and Venezuela were trained in Costa Rica. Medical supplies and weapons were smuggled into Sandinista camps from Venezuela, Panama, Mexico, Costa Rica and—of course—Cuba. A CIA memo of 1979, for example, detailed that over 300 FSLN rebels had received intensive training in Cuba. On several occasions, the CIA noted, large crates of Cuban contraband went to the Sandinistas. These included Soviet AK-47 rifles, 30 caliber machine guns, mortars, anti-tank and anti-aircraft weapons.

In a unique "secret session" of Congress (the first in over one-hundred years) in July 1979, former Representative Robert E. Bauman (R.-Md.) called his colleagues together in a hushed delineation of the extent of international and Cuban support for the FSLN. Tons of ammunition and supplies, Bauman noted, were routinely shipped for delivery into Nicaragua via way stations in Panama, Venezuela and Costa Rica. Up to five daily flights were recorded on certain days, in an intense build-up against the fading Somoza government.

Assistance also came from the Palestine Liberation Organization (PLO). At least twelve planeloads of supplies and arms came from the PLO during several stages of the revolution. Relations between the PLO and the FSLN even had a seal of formality about them when, in Mexico City early in the revolution, the two organizations met and signed a transnational agreement to provide "mutual support." FSLN cadres were also trained in Lebanon, Libya and Algeria under PLO guidance.

Informal support for the Sandinistas came from several Latin American countries. Panama provided a haven for FSLN exiles. Venezuela gave refuge for FSLN terrorists wanted by the Nicaraguan authorities. Costa Rica provided more than $3 million worth of help for recuperating Sandinista guerrillas.

Using Costa Rica as a sanctuary, Cubans, Panamanians, East Germans and other international brigades even took part in the final offensive against Somoza in June 1979. By then, the FSLN movement had grown from a few hundred to about 4,000.

The Sandinista revolution, therefore, was both an "inside" and "outside" job. While both elements were crucial, it was still the guerrillas in the mountains and the cities plus Somoza's own deepening crises that really toppled his government. Somoza, after all, had 12,000 soldiers of his own, and these were also armed and trained outside of Nicaragua—by the USA. This time, however, American foreign policy gave him little help.

After its initial wave of enthusiasm to expose the harsh side of Somoza's government, the U.S. tentatively began to back off. In June 1978 President Carter sent Somoza a letter congratulating him for certain promises he made to restore human rights in Nicaragua. At the same time, the U.S. was delaying military assistance. Washington's two-sided policies confused practically everybody. The FSLN interpreted the Carter letter as a sign that the U.S. was still committed to the government. To Somoza, the letter indicated a lack of clear policy direction by the United States.

The "group of twelve" that had united against Somoza was pushed leftward. They concluded that the idea of using the U.S. to help remove Somoza peaceably was impossible. The result was the creation of the "Broad Opposition Front," a coalition of all anti-government parties and labor unions. They called a general strike and demanded Somoza's resignation. He ignored both.

The month of August was the worst in Somoza's presidency to that time. On the 22nd, a group of twenty-five uniformed Sandinistas, led by Eden Pastora, marched boldly into downtown Managua and openly seized the National Palace, while the Congress was still meeting. They held 1,500 persons hostage, including the Minister of Interior and the President's own cousin. Their demands called for the release of political prisoners and safe passage out of the country.

Within two days a frustrated President Somoza was forced—again—into a new international humiliation. The Sandinistas were raced off to the airport for the flight to Panama on streets lined with waving crowds. Somoza had suffered another serious blow to his prestige.

The audacity of the act captured the public's imagination and moved the Sandinistas into the forefront of the anti-Somoza war. In a time of revolution, extremism almost always prevails over moderation. Nicaragua was no exception.

On the 29th of August, the President faced an internal disorder inside the *Guardia*. An attempted *putsch,* apparently, had been caught just in time. Somoza announced the arrest of twelve senior officers and 200 men. His "house" was beginning to fall apart, from all sides.

September was another bad month. The Sandinistas opened full-scale civil war by attacking the *Guardia* in several cities simultaneously. Mass rebellion occurred in Leon, Estili, Chinandega and Granada. FSLN membership expanded to nearly 1,000 guerrillas. They seized and held the center of several cities, while the *Guardia* had to use the Air Force to remove them.

Somoza ordered heavy airborne attacks, followed by mobile ground assaults. This process was arduous, brutal and slow. The FAN bombings destroyed the central quarters of important urban areas. It took three weeks and over 3,000 casualties, many of them civilians, before the guerrillas and hundreds of new recruits moved up into the interior mountains.

Martial law was imposed once more, and heavy fighting occurred on both sides of the Costa Rican border. In November, Costa Rica broke relations with Nicaragua after the *Guardia* had crossed the border in "hot pursuit" of the fleeing Sandinistas.

Overt support for the beleaguered Somoza government, however, began coming in. El Salvador, Honduras and Guatemala, all of them facing insurrections of their own, gave various moral and material aid to President Somoza. U.S. policy, on the other hand, stiffened against him, but not to the point yet of publicly demanding his immediate resignation.

A large group of conservative Senators and Congressmen from both parties wrote a letter to President Carter demanding that he end his "cold hostility" to Somoza. Statements from Representatives Bauman and John Murphy, Senator Helms and others pointed out the communist influence in the FSLN. To no avail. The Carter Administration began seeking a long-term alternative to Somoza. But they did not want, on the other hand, a Sandinista victory. Belatedly, the U.S. found itself caught between the dilemma of the Somoza-Sandinista struggle for power in Nicaragua.

The Administration applied pressure on the International Monetary Fund to block emergency loans to Nicaragua. Washington formally refused further military aid and coerced other nations, such as Belgium, Israel and Guatemala, into doing the same.

In private negotiations, the Administration asked for Somoza's resignation in favor of an interim government composed of the Broad

Opposition Front and the Liberal Party. Somoza would have to free all political prisoners and leave the country while the Organization of American States (OAS) supervised the elections. He refused, and President Carter recalled over half of the official U.S. representation in Nicaragua. But in retrospect, it was already too late for a political solution. By the beginning of 1979, neither the Somozas nor the Sandinistas were able to compromise. The Civil War was already full-scale.

In June 1979 the FSLN guerrillas quit their hit-and-run tactics and formed together for a final and direct military push against the government. Within weeks, they were strong enough to control most of the major cities and countryside, plus half of Managua. U.S. policy panicked in the face of FSLN military successes and formally called for Somoza's resignation in favor of a broadly-based government backed up by an OAS peacekeeping force. But it was way too late to ignore military realities in the field.

On June 17, the Sandinistas—virtually assured of victory—announced their own five-member *junta*. Facing the inevitable, Washington's solutions grew even more hurried and unrealistic. The U.S. asked that the FSLN share power with a more moderate opposition, a solution the Sandinistas indignantly rejected.

In a last-ditch effort to prevent what it termed "another Cuba," the U.S. then tried to save the *Guardia Nacional* by forcing Somoza to leave immediately. In a telephone call between Somoza and Deputy Secretary of State Warren Christopher, and in a letter from Secretary of State Cyrus Vance, Somoza was told bluntly to leave the country. Under this last-ditch effort, the U.S. would then extend aid to the *Guardia* and recognize a *junta* of FSLN and other opposition groups. Somoza left for Miami on July 17, but the U.S. solution fell instantly, like a house of cards.

On July 19 the victorious FSLN entered Managua. Within twenty-four hours the *Guardia* disintegrated altogether. The Sandinistas appointed Tomás Borge as the head of the police, and quickly drove out the nominal head of the transition government. The Somoza era was over, the Sandinista era had begun.

The New Sandinistas

The essential historic difference between the Sandinistas and the Somozas is systemic. The victory of the FSLN in 1979 reversed more than a century of *caudillo* politics inherited from colonial Spain. The Somozas were probably the last of the *caudillo*-authoritarians in Nicaraguan history; the Sandinistas certainly are the first of the ideological-totalitarians. In political system and culture, the difference is a great watershed between the Old Right and the New Left.

Augusto Sandino himself was also a product of the old regime—despite his flair for publicity and his international acclaim. He was an old-fashioned guerrilla, but his namesakes today are truly "modern." By comparison, Sandino was also a *caudillo,* as were individual members of the Chamorro family, which spent most of its public life in a losing effort against the Somoza family. But the family system appears to be gone forever. If the FSLN fulfills its own revolutionary momentum, Nicaragua will never be the same.

The Sandinistas have introduced twentieth century methods of indoctrination and social control in an attempt to dominate today's Nicaragua in a manner that Anastasio Somoza could never entertain. In the short space of two years, they have imported thousands of Soviet, Cuban and other international "advisors"—including the PLO—to remold the old-style Nicaraguan system into a potential Central American "behemoth" state, in the style of Fidel Castro's Cuba. As in totalitarian Cuba, the Sandinistas have already set up neighborhood associations as local spy networks for the government.

The Sandinistas have made no bones about their intentions to transform Nicaragua into a socialistic and militaristic bureaucratic state. Official government press releases are nearly always full of the commonplace jargon of Marxist ideology. Such statements could have easily come from Cuba or the Soviet bloc, in a repetition of themes which have been familiar to western observers for decades: anti-imperialism, anti-capitalism, worker and Third World solidarity, etc. Government leaders openly refer to Nicaragua as a "people's democracy." This is an ideological regime, a novelty in Central American history.

The Sandinistas have also backed up their words with deeds. Even if they do not openly admit it, the FSLN is a political party, and Marxist-Leninist to the core. Today, the FSLN controls practically everything in the country. Mass organizations belong to them, as does the army, the police, most of the labor unions and media. In practically every arena, they have outdone Somoza by a long shot. Somoza may have been a dictator, but he did not fall from power because he was too ruthless and powerful. He fell because of weakness; because he *lost* his power. The Sandinistas, apparently, do not intend to make the same mistake.

Past the second anniversary of the Sandinista revolution, today's Nicaragua makes only a token pretention of political freedom. The free elections promised by the government have not materialized. All campaigning has been banned for at least two years, and the elections— originally scheduled for 1981—will not take place until at least 1985, if at all. There is widespread doubt that the elections will ever materialize. Unlike the Somoza government, the FSLN does not even pretend to include democracy as a serious political objective.

Under the Sandinista theories of Marxism-Leninism, the concept of democracy has nothing in common with free elections and political pluralism. The FSLN, they say, is the "vanguard" of the people.

Elections are considered superfluous. *Junta* member Sergio Ramírez proclaimed the Sandinista version of democracy when he said, "The elections that took place with rifles in Nicaragua were the most authentic in all of Latin America." Council of State member Federico López told the Nicaraguan people on Managua radio that "popular" democracy is ruling Nicaragua. This concept, he explained, occurs when "the working classes have organized their revolutionary power in the new state and in many economic, social and political organizations. Because these instruments are the people's power, they are democratic, more democratic than any other state instrument of the capitalists and the oppressors."

"Revolutionary" democracy in the new Nicaragua was demonstrated clearly on July 19, 1981 when *Junta* coordinator Daniel Ortega orchestrated a massive crowd of hundreds of thousands of Sandinista supporters in a Managua "popular assembly." Over and over again, Ortega read decrees to the throng, asking them over microphones "Is this assembly in agreement with this measure," to which the croud responded with deafening "yeas." Shades of the Robespierrian Thermidor![23]

Nicaraguan "democracy" will be rooted in mass organizations, or the neighborhood associations patterned on the Cuban model. The only technical concession the Sandinistas make to the notion of political liberty is the nominal existence of six other political parties, of which five oppose the FSLN. Although politicians who form these parties are forbidden to campaign for political office, the parties are permitted to advertise and to hold membership drives. But the Sandinistas harrass them all along the line. Mobs organized by the government and the police have repeatedly terrorized the opposition. The Nicaraguan Democratic Party, for example, was forced by organized and mass violence to cancel two major rallies in 1981. The Democratic Conservative Party has met the same fate.

The structure of political power is much different from the *personalismo* style of the past. The structure at the top is a bureaucratic jungle. Nine Sandinista "commanders," most of them civil war veterans, comprise the Directorate. Together they wield executive power, but each commander has his own individual ministry.

Next to the Directorate is the *Junta,* now down to three members (from five). Daniel Ortega is the leading member of the *Junta* and is also a member of the Directorate. Sergio Ramírez Mercado, another Sandinista, is the second Junta member, while Rafael Córdova Rivas, from the Democratic Conservative Party, is the third member. Córdova Rivas is the only remaining non-Marxist and non-FSLN member of either the Directorate or the Junta. Previous members of the *Junta* who resigned were Arturo Cruz, who left to become Ambassador to the U.S.; Violeta Chamorro, the widow of the assassinated *La Prensa* editor; Alfonso

Robelo, a millionaire businessman; and Moisés Hassán, now Minister of Construction.

Below the *Junta* are the Ministries, but the posts are held by Directorate members. The political network, indeed, is interlocking. Minor Ministries, however, are held by three Catholic priests (of a Marxist bent) and several civilians. The top posts are all Directorate members: Tomás Borge (Interior), Humberto Ortega (Defense), Jaime Wheelock (Agriculture) and Henry Ruíz (Planning).

Beyond the ministries is a 52-member Council of State—in reality a rubber stamp Congress which has no more authentic power than what the *Junta* and Directorate give to it. Twelve non-Marxist members of this body have already boycotted it in protest against the government's refusal to grant real political freedom.

The complexity of the FSLN governmental structure has so far prevented the emergence of a single dominant figure. It remains to be seen for just how long nine men can continue to govern as a body. To be sure, the Directorate has its own factions, but their policy debates have centered upon the pace and tactics of change toward Marxist socialism, not the *nature* of the change, and certainly not the *direction* Nicaragua has been heading.

The lessons of history, in Nicaragua and elsewhere, holds little real hope for the long-term continuity of group dictatorship. In the Communist systems of Eastern Europe and the U.S.S.R., for example, the Ministry of Interior has frequently played the key role. In Nicaragua, that is Tomás Borge, the last of the original Sandinistas still in the government.

The political situation, therefore, contains the seeds of instability. This would be even more the case were it not for the Sandinista use of thousands of Soviet-bloc and Cuban technicians and military advisors. Sandinista rule has been shored-up considerably by outsiders. Today's Nicaragua, indeed, is a regional beachhead of international communism. This fact alone makes the FSLN movement a revolution of historic proportions, not just a coup in the Central American tradition.

The New Nicaragua

At the newly named Augusto Sandino airport a common sight in the last year has been the Soviet-built Aeroflot Tupolev jetliners, on loan to Cubana Airlines. These monsters symbolize the new Nicaragua. The Sandinistas have lined up solidly behind the "socialist camp," under the political smokescreen of "non-alignment." They have signed large-scale military and technical agreements with the U.S.S.R. and East Germany. FSLN leaders have made historic trips to visit the titans of the communist world: Leonid Brezhnev, Kim Il Sung, etc.

Almost immediately after taking power in 1979, FSLN leaders went to Moscow to sign a rare party-to-party accord with the Soviet Communist Party. The next year they solidified their relations with the PLO when Yassar Arafat visited Managua and opened a center of operations, in effect a PLO embassy. Fidel Castro visited Managua to make the keynote speech at the first anniversary of the 1979 revolution.

There is no doubt that the Havana-Managua "axis" is a Caribbean-Central American reality. This has changed the entire picture of regional politics. Within two months after the revolution, the FSLN brought in over 1,200 Cuban teachers and technicians in a massive work-indoctrination program. The figure is now (1982) up to over 5,000.

There are now more Cubans in Nicaragua than there were ever American Marines, even during the guerrilla war against Sandino. Considering Cuba's relatively small population, plus its thousands of troops in Africa, this is truly an astounding commitment. The new regime in Nicaragua is also doing its part to help Castro in Africa, where 500 Nicaraguan troops are reported fighting alongside Cuban troops in Angola.

Nicaragua is now a major base of operations for the guerrilla war in El Salvador. Tons of arms have been flown to El Salvador in clandestine airlifts through Nicaragua. Training camps in Nicaragua have been set up for Salvadoran guerrillas. Most of the commanders of these camps were trained in Cuba or the Soviet Union. Nicaraguans are reported to be fighting for the Salvadoran rebels, but the precise numbers are not publicly known.

The build-up of Cuban-Soviet military power inside Nicaragua is unprecedented in Central American history. The Sandinistas are turning the country into a major strategic arms depot. The Sandinista army presently has about 30,000 trained personnel and has plans to expand to 50,000 men, almost five times the size of the old *Guardia Nacional*. The ready reserve number about 30,000 and the popular militia another 30,000. Thus Nicaragua has about 90,000 men under arms. This is considerably larger than the combined armies of the rest of Central America.

The new citizen militia will be a huge operation if it succeeds as planned. The Sandinistas are training the militia to number about 250,000 men and women, a full 10 percent of the population. All high school and college students have been told that it is their revolutionary "duty" to join the militia.

About 30 Soviet-built tanks have been shipped into the country. Nicaragua has also received mortars, howitzers, antomatic rifles, heavy artillery, anti-aircraft guns and armored personnel carriers. Aircraft runways in several areas of the country are being improved in order to handle MIG 17 and MIG 21 Soviet-made fighters. The Sandinistas have also built 27 new military bases inside the country.

Even now, the Nicaraguan military far exceeds any traditional or standard necessity. It is already a potent tool for the Castro-backed "export" of revolution, not to mention its obvious utility against internal dissidence.

Dissent against the government has grown increasingly during the two years of Sandinista rule. The tragedy of the Miskito Indians of the east coast is particularly brutal. Thousands of these Indians have chosen exile in Honduras rather than endure hardships imposed upon them from Managua.

Armed clashes with the Sandinista authorities killed or wounded over 100 Indians in the first two years after the revolution, causing a wave of rioting and unrest throughout the Atlantic seaboard. There were numerous reports citing the branding and torturing of Miskitos living near the Honduran border in order to keep them from leaving the country. In the town of Bluefields, an anti-government riot resulted in a full-scale Sandinista military occupation. Local leaders were beaten, and their homes were searched.

But the worst was still to come. In December 1981 through February 1982, the Miskito Indians were the victims of what has been called Latin America's single greatest human rights violation in recent history. The government embarked on a massive resettlement program, attacking several unarmed Indian communities and forcing their inhabitants into Nicaragua's interior.

The Indians' Council of Elders reported that 42 villages were firebombed and 49 churches destroyed. Sandinista troops took some Miskitos from their homes at night, lined them up and shot them one by one. A pregnant woman and her child were burned alive. Thirty-five persons in the village of Leymus were buried alive. Thousands were imprisoned or reported missing after having been seen in the hands of security forces. As many as 20,000 Indians fled for their lives across the border into Honduras.[24]

Over 200,000 other Nicaraguans are said to have left the country in protest against the increasingly rigid government in Managua. Many exiled leaders have a long history of anti-Somoza politics and some, like Eden Pastora (*Commandante Cero*), were prominent Sandinistas themselves. The revolution is beginning to devour its own children.

José Francisco Cardenal is one. He spent seven months in a Somoza jail and was named Vice President of the Council of State under the Sandinistas. Today, he is a fierce opponent of the regime and is a leader of the Nicaraguan Democratic Union, a movement which is actively seeking to overthrow the FSLN.

Another exile leader is Jaime Pasquier, who resigned as the Nicaraguan Ambassador to the United Nations in Geneva, Switzerland and sought political asylum in the United States. "What exists in Nicaragua is a complete dictatorship," he told a Council for Inter-American Security meeting in July 1981. "They are hoping to get economic help. After that, they will declare Nicaragua a communist country."[25]

Perhaps the most prominent and dangerous foe of the Sandinistas is Fernando Chamorro, cousin of the late editor of *La Prensa*. As the latest in a long line of Chamorros, Fernando Chamorro's credentials go way back. In 1959, he participated in a movement against Luis Somoza headed by his cousin, Pedro Joaquín Chamorro. He later spent several years in exile and was imprisoned by Anastasio Somoza several times. Fernando gained international attention in 1979 when he climbed to the top of Managua's Hotel Intercontinental and fired a bazooka into Somoza's headquarters. He fought aside Eden Pastora on the southern front during the civil war and attained the rank of Commander of the General Staff of the FSLN.

Today, Fernando Chamorro is again in exile against his government. In July 1981 he escaped from Nicaragua and, two weeks later, was named Commander-in-Chief of the Revolutionary Nicaraguan Armed Forces. This group has already begun military operations against the Sandinistas and has proclaimed its intentions to topple the regime in the same mountains that the FSLN had its own start. A "freedom force" of over 600 ex-*Guardia* soldiers and other exiles is being eassembled in Honduras for this very purpose. "The hills are alive again" with the recurrent echoes of Augusto Sandino's ghosts. But opposition from without has not stopped the Sandinistas from their drive for absolute internal control.

At the very beginnings of Sandinista rule, a tight clamp was placed on the press. Private broadcasting licenses were revoked, stories were censored, publishing houses were closed, and several journalists were arrested. Equal restrictions have been placed on television and radio. During the first six months, only one radio station and one television station were allowed to operate. All media personnel had to join one of two unions, both Sandinista controlled. These restrictions continue today. Opposition groups may buy radio time, but only at the government's disposal.

The print media is a different picture, but only slightly. The Chamorro family still monopolizes the newspaper chain, as they did under the Somoza government, and *La Prensa* still attacks the government regularly. But they are no happier today than they have ever been. Pedro J. Chamorro, Jr., son of the late *La Prensa* editor, has come down on the government hard, just as his father—and *his* father before *him*—did against Somoza. Constantly harassed by Sandinista-led mobs against his newspaper, he described to reporters the true nature of the Sandinista regime:

They do not grant freedom of assembly to all parties—only to the Sandinistas.

They stop all others from meeting. They have confiscated many industries in the private sector—including some not owned by the Somozas. They have attacked all the independent media.

71

They have established close connections with the Soviet Union. They practically idolize Cuba. They say that someone needs to teach us "the Cuban way." They regard Fidel Castro as if he were the leader of the world.

They have created a climate of hate. The Nicaraguan revolution was a united effort of all classes to get rid of a dictatorship. Class hatred started only after the revolution. Now the bourgeoisie feels threatened and doesn't want to invest. There has been a brain drain. This revolution is not democratic.

Asked about the differences between the old regime and the old one, the younger Chamorro was candid:

Neither better nor worse. Under Somoza there were times when there was no freedom whatever; there were journalists in jail; there were armed attacks on our building at night. There were two and a half years of strict press censorship. My father was in jail several times before he was killed. Now the situation is different.

The problem is that the Government wants us to say there is complete freedom of the press. But we cannot violate our principles; we have to speak the truth. If officials want us to say there is complete press freedom they should get rid of the restrictions. Our Constitution guarantees freedom of the press.[26]

La Prensa has a paid circulation of 75,000, still much more than the official Sandinista newspaper, *La Barricada.* But the tradition continues! *La Barricada* is also owned by a Chamorro, Pedro Joaquín's son, Carlos. Another newspaper, the pro-Sandinista *El Nuevo Diario,* is directed by Pedro Joaquín Chamorro's brother, Xavier.

The Sandinistas have drafted a new law governing the press which would provide penalties for infractions including fines of $2,500 and suspensions of the guilty media. The Ibero-American Federation of Journalist Associations declared that the proposed press law responds to a "totalitarian concept" of information. *La Prensa* co-editor Pedro J. Chamorro, Jr. told a meeting of the Inter American Press Association in March: "If only ten per cent of this bill is passed, I think it will be the end to the remnants of freedom of the press that still survive in Nicaragua."[27]

The government declared a 30-day "state of emergency" on March 15, 1982 and imposed total censorship on *La Prensa.* Newspapers were required to submit copies to authorities before they could be distributed to newsstands. All independent radio broadcasting was suspended, and radio stations were required to carry government-generated programming.

Even in a revolution, some things never change. But change—toward the worst—is the essence of today's Nicaragua. The labor unions are a case in point. The Sandinista Workers Federation has for months campaigned to undercut the other labor unions and force the consolidation of all unions into one organization controlled by the FLSN. Strikes are strictly forbidden.

The Catholic Church (minus the radical priests within the government) has vigorously protested the nature of the regime. Whatever opposition is allowed has rallied around Managua's Archbishop, Miguel Obando y Bravo. The Sandinista practice of sending hundreds of Nicaraguan youth to atheist Cuba for schooling has particularly irked the Church hierarchy. Over 1,000 youngsters have been exported to Cuba for this reason. Marxist indoctrination in the country's educational system is another major concern. The Catholic hierarchy of Nicaragua has officially accused the Sandinistas of trying to turn the country into a "Marxist-Atheist" nation.

They are right. The country is also being fashioned into a socialist economy. In early 1980, many important industries were nationalized: banks, insurance companies, all the old Somoza holdings—in total, more than 400 companies. Somoza may have been rich, but the new government—collectively—has more than he ever had. The government has confiscated all land that was rented by owners holding over 850 acres in certain parts of the country, 1700 in other parts.

The government, however, faces a severe shortage of foreign exchange. More critical in the long run is the erosion of the nation's productive base, particularly if foreign investment continues to lag. A recent study concluded that it would take seven years for the *per capita* output of goods and services to reach the 1978 level. "Unless something happens," one economist predicted, "we're talking about the long-term running down of Nicaragua's economy."[28]

The country already owes almost $3 billion to foreign creditors, a debt which increases at the rate of $2.5 million per day. A one year state of "economic and social emergency" was decreed in September 1981. Foreign currency reserves are practically gone, in spite of the fact that Nicaragua received nearly $450 million in aid and grants in 1981. The private sector is completely dominated by the government, a system reminiscent of Mussolini's "corporate" state economy.

Nicaraguan businessmen who formed the Superior Council for Private Enterprise (COSEP) had their leaders imprisoned in October 1981. COSEP's Vice-President, Jorge Salazar, had already been shot to death by security forces months earlier at a Managua gas station. Many COSEP leaders who escaped the FSLN security police were forced into exile. On October 27th a mob of Sandinista youth attacked the home of businessman Alfonso Robelo, who is President of the Nicaraguan Democratic Movement. So much for private enterprise in revolutionary Nicaragua!

Investment and foreign aid into Nicaragua depends to a great degree upon the "climate" that the Sandinistas offer to outsiders. Today's climate could hardly be worse. President Somoza was viciously accused of countless human rights abuses, especially by his detractors in the

United States. But in today's Nicaragua the climate has gone from bad to worse.

During the rule of Somoza I, there was a running commentary that there were two political prisoners in Nicaragua, and one was held because he criticized President Roosevelt. Hyperbole aside, that story highlights the essential difference between the two regimes. In revolutionary Nicaragua, political prisoners symbolize politics. By May 1980 there were over 12,000, at least half of whom were former members of Somoza's *Guardia National*. Hundreds of these were killed outright by Sandinista firing squads. With all of his excesses—and his problems from the opposition—Somoza never even dared approach this level. Today's prisoners actually outnumber the size of Somoza's old *Guardia*.

Conditions in Nicaragua's prisons are grim, and prisoners are frequently held without public trial. Prisoners are ill-fed and poorly clothed, as the following U.S. State Department *Countries Report* testifies:

> Prisons in Nicaragua are overcrowded, and conditions are generally inadequate by international standards. The standard diet for detainees is poor in nutrients and health facilities are extremely limited. The conditions reflect the living standards of the population. . . The government has publicly admitted that abuses do occur.[29]

When the Sandinistas declared a 30-day "state of emergency" on March 15, 1982, they suspended the right of *habeas corpus* along with other rights to engage in trade union organizing and political activities and freedoms of press and assembly. The government has also decreed that officials and prominent opposition politicians and businessmen may not leave the country.

Opposition leaders worried that the state of emergency might be extended beyond 30 days, establishing permanent censorship and maintaining restrictions on the freedom to criticize the government. "This could be one more step in the radicalization of the regime," said Jaime Chamorro, manager of *La Prensa*. "I suspect that the only real reason for the state of emergency is to censor *La Prensa*."[30] Days after the imposition of the state of emergency, the government suspended publication of *La Prensa* for the seventh time since the Sandinista takeover.

The *Wall Street Journal* reacted to Nicaragua's state of emergency with an editorial on March 19 entitled "Nicaragua Makes It Official":

> Nicaragua, like Poland, has finally made it official: It has declared itself a police state. . .There is, of course, no surprise in any of this. It follows the classic pattern of Marxist revolutionaries everywhere. First destabilize the society, then masquerade as social democrats while seizing power with armed force, then declare that emergency conditions make it necessary to "mobilize" society, i.e., impose totalitarian conditions. The script was written in 1917, it worked well in Eastern Europe and Cuba, and now we are seeing it in Central America.

It is an irony of history that the Somoza government was singled out from so many quarters for its human rights violations. Certainly these occurred, especially during the civil war and the numerous attempted coups against his government. But the Sandinistas—who took on revolution and civil war allegedly to correct these violations—have proven to be much worse in practice. In the meantime, the long-suffering people of Nicaragua, who have gone from despot to despot, from revolution to revolution, must now endure a form of tyranny even more institutionalized than before, and even more solidly supported by external tyrannies of the same kind. At least during the American era, the dominant outside influence made honest attempts to promote political civility and justice.

In the absence of a dominant American voice, and considering the sad political history of Nicaragua, the future holds little promise for the triumph of democracy in that troubled country. Reminiscent of Nazi Germany, Radio Sandino told its listeners on June 20, 1981 that "the Sandinista Revolution was not designed to last one or two years. It was designed to last forever."[31]

VII. CONCLUSION: RETROSPECT AND PROSPECT

Retrospect

In August 1909 a small force of U.S. Marines landed on Nicaragua's east coast, thus beginning nearly three-quarters of a century of involved relations between the two countries. This relationship has swayed back and forth, under good and bad times, during the continuing turbulence of the Twentieth Century. Indeed, it is fair to say that both countries have contributed to this turbulence themselves, if only in a small measure, by the nature of their relationship. Many of these years were truly stormy ones, including the present.

The dynamics of the United States and Nicaragua in history have been magnified by the growing alignment of the FSLN with Cuba and Russia and its hostility toward the U.S. The strategic and geopolitical asymmetries between the two societies makes any Nicaraguan "escape" from the American shadow, however, ultimately impossible.

Nicaragua may pretend a diplomatic "neutralism," or like Cuba, she may come under the full weight of Soviet intervention in Latin America. But there is no possible way for Nicaragua to ignore the realities of American power in Latin America, even if that power is exercised negatively or from a political distance. That certainly is one of the obvious lessons of history.

Another lesson of the past, although probably not so obvious, shows that American power contains inherent limitations. Whereas the U.S. came to assume a strategic and geopolitical hegemony over Central America, Washington has never been strong enough—or willing enough—to exercise a lasting form of hemispheric "colonialism." The occupation of Nicaragua in the early decades of the century was tentative, frustrating and historically brief. It was done for strategic reasons, and when Washington became too involved in local issues, espe-

77

cially the guerrilla war against Sandino, the U.S. wasted little time getting out as fast as conditions permitted.

By the definition of its own political culture and strategic demands, therefore, the U.S. became satisfied if the region stayed content under the strategic umbrella of the American Navy. Against Germany and Japan, this was all that Washington asked of Nicaragua, and that's all she got in return. It was an alliance of unequals, and it served both national interests.

For its part, Nicaragua played the American "card" very well. The Somozas were the acknowledged masters of this. They all depended upon American nonintervention, at the very least. Diplomatic recognition was a minimal essential; assistance and cordiality were even better. But no government could survive a determined U.S. opposition, and all knew it. They took cunning advantage of U.S. foreign policy, particularly the growing American concern with world communism.

During World War II and the Cold War, Nicaragua was America's best ally, and the U.S. was the Somoza's best lever against domestic political opposition. The two served each other well, as long as the tacit alliance lasted. When it fell apart during the Carter Administration, the whole roof caved in, on both the Somoza dynasty and on Central American stability.

The reliance of the U.S. on the Somoza family may not have been ideal from a theoretical and critical perspective, but there was a built-in historic and strategic reason for it. That reason served over four decades of American diplomacy.

Americans of this period were well aware that they were not really promoting liberal democracy by helping to shore up the Somoza government. But they were also wise enough to realize that they couldn't do this anyway, despite the best of intentions. They understood that if Somoza fell, another "strong man" would only take his place. Certainly, there was nothing in the Conservative opposition, or in Nicaragua's history, to give any other answer.

The Conservatives in power were historically just as determined to stay in, by hook or by crook, as the Liberals were. They raised their own private armies. They organized their own plots, coups and revolutions. They were as violent as the Liberals, and were no less willing to use bribery and patronage to keep political power. During the 1916-25 period it was the Conservative Chamorro family that earned the world's notoriety as Nicaragua's "dictators." Out of power, the Chamorros proved just as violently rebellious as the Liberals were before them.

Modern-day critics of Somoza's human rights abuses may console themselves in the smug moralism of their cause, but their onesided campaign against the government and the *Guardia* makes these Americans no less ignorant of Nicaragua than the legions of reformers in the past. The result is the same type of "cultural gap" that erroneously directed much of early-century U.S. policy.

The terrorism and revolutionary violence which almost continuously beset the Nicaraguan government was rooted deep within the political system. But in choosing to systematically downgrade or deny the Marxist-Leninist nature of the present Sandinistas, Carter Administration officials and the liberal media were themselves guilty of an morally shallow bias. This bias played a significant role in the eventual downfall of the Somoza government. True to the past, the replacement is worse still for the Nicaraguan people and for Western interests.

But in a deeper sense, Somoza's critics were also Nicaragua's critics, much as the Somozas were the products of the culture they inherited. In reality, the Nicaraguan political system was a "warfare" system, dynamically geared toward a near constancy of palace intrigue, coup and armed uprising. But it was not a repressive system in the classic sense, and neither widespread torture nor systematic political detention, in the Castro style, were used. Somoza's Nicaragua was "authoritarian," not "totalitarian."

But in the final analysis, it made little difference which party or ruler was in power, just as long as there was power. In Nicaragua's history, there was little room in the middle between the *caudillo* and anarchy. The Marines may have provided some middle ground, but this was both temporal and artificial. Nicaragua's history and political culture proved more lasting than either the Marine Corps or the U.S. State Department.

In retrospect, finally, the Carter Administration must share a large part of the blame for the fall of Nicaragua into the hands of a Sandinista-communist regime deeply hostile to the U.S. and aligned with Cuba and the USSR. The replacement of the Somozas with the Sandinistas has shifted the diplomatic balance in Central American significantly leftward. The psychological and material lift this gives to other revolutionary movements in the region will haunt U.S. policy for many years to come. It has already caused considerable trouble.

With its blind and amateurish zeal to uncover human rights sins of the Somoza government, its single-minded targeting of Somoza, with the glaring double standard which that implied, and by its tardy confusion and lack of strategic direction, the Administration of Jimmy Carter mishandled the Nicaragua crisis from practically every angle. It will take Central America a long time to recover from his mistakes.

Prospect

The question now remains, what will the Sandinistas ultimately do, now that they have replaced the Somozas? Equally important, how will U.S. policy help continue to shape the national interest, with a new system installed in Managua? After two years, the prognosis is by no means obvious.

The extent of the Sandinista revolution is deep. They have changed both the internal and external nature of the nation's politics in a profound way. Never before has the U.S. been faced with such anti-American rhetoric and policy from Nicaragua. Never before has the domestic picture in Nicaragua been so decidedly shaped by a determined mix of ideologically-motivated revolutionaries.

The initial U.S. reaction to the Sandinista triumph was generous. The U.S. voted in the Inter-American Development Bank for all loans proposed to Nicaragua. The Bank gave the Sandinistas, in nineteen months of the Carter Administration, almost twice the amount of money it gave the Somoza government in the nineteen previous years ($134 million from 1960 to mid-1979; $262 million from mid-1979 to 1981)! The U.S. bilateral aid program was also generous, but much more controversial. A $75 million economic aid bill became the most explosive foreign policy issue in the 1980 Congress. Anti-Sandinista factions of Congressmen led a determined battle against the package, accusing the Carter Administration of "selling out" to the Managua "Castroites."

As evidence of the strong Cuban presence kept coming in, the aid program grew more embarrassing for President Carter. House Speaker "Tip" O'Neill postponed the vote, but he could not delay it forever. The final version, however, was watered down considerably by House Republicans, who sucessfully passed ten amendments which, in effect, attached serious strings to the allocation of U.S. assistance.

Although the aid program passed, Nicaragua continued to dominate Latin American policy in Congress. The escalating guerrilla wars in El Salvador and Guatemala made Central America the new Cold War arena. Daily headlines from Central America made Americans more attuned to the news of the region.

Nicaragua was crucial to this. Once again, Americans were hearing of Sandinistas, and what they heard was decidedly anti-U.S. Statements from Junta leaders, such as the following one made in North Korea by Tomás Borge, did the Carter conciliatory policy little benefit:

> The Nicaraguan revolutionaries will not be content until the imperialists have been overthrown in all parts of the world. The imperialist United States should not believe that they are to rule South Korea permanently. . .We stand with the forces of peace and progress, which are the socialist countries. Our strategic goal is clear, our principles are clear, too.[32]

Defense Minister Humberto Ortega, in a speech published in August 1981, also left no doubt about the political character of the new regime, when he proclaimed that:

> "Without Sandinism we cannot be Marxist-Leninist, and Sandinism without Marxism-Leninism cannot be revolutionary. That is why they are indissolubly united, and that is why our moral force is Sandinism, our political force is Sandinism, and our doctrine is Marxism-Leninism."

80

Denouncing the United States' "perverse and slanderous anti-communist propaganda," Ortega explained that the world is divided into two camps: "on one side the camp of imperialism, the camp of capitalism headed by the United States and the rest of the capitalist countries of Europe and of the world, and on the other side the socialist camp, composed of distinct countries of Europe, Asia, and Latin America, with the Soviet Union as their vanguard." Ortega made it plain that Nicaragua is now in what he called the "socialist" camp.[33]

Although Latin America played almost no role in the 1980 presidential election, Ronald Reagan's charges that the Carter Administration was "weak" in foreign policy was, in large part, tied to the deterioration of U.S. interests in Central America. In the middle of this deterioration was Nicaragua, and from the beginning, the new Administration made it clear that a stronger approach was in the making.

Despite the fact that the FSLN leadership had a 19-year history of close ties to Cuba, the dominant view of the Carter Administration was that economic and political pluralism was still salvageable in Nicaragua, provided that Washington extended a benevolent hand. The Reagan Administration is deeply skeptical of this, and their policies have not been nearly so naive. The expansion of violence in El Salvador and the persuasive evidence of a Sandinista-Cuban role in this compelled the Reagan State Department, in March 1981, to suspend further economic and food assistance. These would not continue, Washington stated clearly, unless there was a marked decline in Sandinista help to the rebels in El Salvador.

But the terrorism and strife in Central America has continued, and official reports have noted a similar continuation of Nicaraguan support to the leftist guerrillas in El Salvador. Assistant Secretary of State for Inter-American Affairs Thomas Enders underscored the Administration's hard line in his first official visit to Nicaragua in August 1981. With unusual bluntness, Enders was reported to have told the Sandinista Directorate that the United States has 100 times the population of Nicaragua, and in any potential crisis, Nicaragua would be the sure loser. The Sandinistas, for their part, supposedly reminded Enders of the futility of the Marine excursions against the first Sandinistas, along with other Vietnam-type scenarios, as if to "freshen" his memory.[34]

The waning months of 1981 saw the Reagan Administration keep a sharp eye on the deterioration in Central America. Public statements by State Department and White House officials have indicated that Washington does not intend to permit a Soviet and Cuban supported wedge to threaten historic U.S. interests in the area. In an OAS meeting at St. Lucia on December 4th, Secretary of State Haig made it clear that there were no current plans for unilateral American troop intervention. In an appeal for possible joint action, however, the Secretary stated that "the United States is prepared to join others in doing what-

81

ever is prudent and necessary to prevent any country in Central America from becoming the platform of terror and war in the region."

Beneath the many public statements from both Managua and Washington, however, private diplomacy went on throughout the last part of 1981. This dialogue involved six meetings between Assistant Secretary Enders and Nicaraguan political leaders.

February and March 1982 saw a flurry of charges and counter-charges between the United States and Nicaragua and shuttle diplomacy by the Mexican Foreign Minister aimed at encouraging a negotiated settlement.

The U.S. State Department sharply criticized the Sandinista regime for supporting insurrections in other countries. Assistant Secretary of State Enders told a Senate subcommittee on February 1 that "Nicaragua is being exploited as a base for the export of subversion and armed intervention throughout Central America."[35] The next day, Secretary of State Alexander Haig said, "All the countries in the Caribbean are confronted by a growing threat from Cuba and its new-found ally, Nicaragua."[36]

The Reagan Administration repeatedly accused the Sandinistas of arming and training the Salvadoran guerrillas and of building a military apparatus more powerful than necessary for national defense. CIA Director William Casey claimed that the insurgency in El Salvador was being run out of Managua and briefed Congressional leaders, reportedly showing them satellite photos demonstrating that extensive supplies of arms were entering El Salvador from Nicaragua and Cuba.[37] The State Department staged an elaborate press briefing on March 9 and showed aerial photographs of new Soviet-style military installations in Managua.

The Sandinistas counter-charged that the United States was preparing to destabilize Nicaragua. The *Washington Post* had run a front page article on March 10 claiming that the Reagan Administration was planning to send a paramilitary force of 500 Latin Americans to conduct covert operations inside Nicaragua, operating under a $19 million CIA budget.[38] The next day, the *New York Times* said that President Reagan had rejected the proposal to finance and support the creation of a paramilitary force in Central America and had, instead, decided to provide financial aid to moderate elements in Nicaragua.[39] But the damage had already been done. The Sandinistas seized on the *Washington Post* report and decreed a state of emergency, declaring that a U.S. invasion was "imminent."[40]

Junta leader Daniel Ortega took the Sandinista charges against the United States to the United Nations Security Council. U.S. Ambassador to the United Nations Jeane Kirkpatrick replied that the assertions were "ridiculous" and said the Nicaraguans were "accusing the United States of the kinds of political behavior of which [Nicaragua] is guilty—large-scale interventions to overthrow neighboring governments."[41]

The Sandinistas were apparently using anti-Yankee rhetoric to cast Nicaragua in the role of underdog, divert domestic attention from the economic disaster at home, and justify ending press freedom and suspending remaining civil and political rights. Not even Interior Minister Tomás Borge took seriously the notion of an "imminent" U.S. invasion. He told a correspondent for London's *The Economist* that there was "relatively little likelihood of an American invasion. It would be very difficult for the United States in the present context of international relations."[42]

Meanwhile, Secretary of State Alexander Haig made five proposals he said could be the basis for a settlement with Nicaragua: (1) the United States and Nicaragua would enter into a non-aggression pact, (2) the United States would agree to curb activities of anti-Sandinista exiles, (3) the Reagan Administration would ask Congress to renew economic assistance to Nicaragua, (4) Nicaragua would agree "to get out of El Salvador, to wind up the command and control, the munitions, ammunition and training camps," and (5) Nicaragua would agree not to import heavy offensive weapons and to reduce the number of foreign military and security advisors in its territory to "a reasonable low level."[43]

It remains to be seen if these proposals go anywhere. The Sandinistas already deny that they supply arms to the Salvadoran guerrillas, and Daniel Ortega at the United Nations rejected the proposed "humiliating" restrictions on the Nicaraguan military. But he said the Nicaraguan government was willing to begin "direct and frank conversations" with the United States.[44]

The two sides are now stalled, separated by political and military differences which, for the moment, appear irrevocable. The core issue remains the Sandinista support for Cuba and for the guerrilla revolution in El Salvador, an issue which promises to keep Central America in turmoil for years to come.

Whether or not a political detente ensues is, at this moment, very doubtful. But the stark reminders of history have at least served to clear the air between the two governments. Still, the future remains uncertain and dangerous.

What is certain, however, is the history between the two countries. In her classic article on "Dictatorships and Double Standards," Professor Jeane Kirkpatrick (now U.N. Ambassador) summarized the confusions that the Carter Administration had with trying to remove Somoza. Her observations would also apply equally to past U.S. Administrations, especially to the early century reformers who thought that made-in-USA political democracy was exportable to Nicaragua's *caudillos*. Her written scenario of 1979 compared Somoza to the Shah of Iran and, true to history, was analyzed, brilliantly, as follows:

But it seems clear that the architects of contemporary American foreign policy have little idea of how to go about encouraging the liberalization of an autocracy. In neither Nicaragua nor Iran did they realize that the only likely result of an effort to replace an incumbent autocrat with one of his moderate critics or a "broad-based coalition" would be to sap the foundations of the existing regime without moving the nation any closer to democracy. Yet this outcome was entirely predictable. Authority in traditional autocracies is transmitted through personal relations: from the ruler to his close associates (relatives, household members, personal friends) and from them to people to whom the associates are related by personal ties resembling their own relation to the ruler. The fabric of authority unravels quickly when the power and status of the man at the top are undermined or eliminated. The longer the autocrat has held power, and the more pervasive his personal influence, the more dependent a nation's institutions will be on him. Without him, the organized life of the society will collapse, like an arch from which the keystone has been removed. The blend of qualities that bound the Iranian army to the Shah or the national guard to Somoza is typical of the relationship—personal, hierarchical, non-transferable—that support a traditional autocracy. The speed with which armies collapse, bureaucracies abdicate, and social structures dissolve once the autocrat is removed frequently surprises American policymakers and journalists accustomed to public institutions based on universalistic norms rather than particularistic relations.[45]

If the Carter Administration, in its enthusiasm to help remove Somoza against deepening domestic and international opposition, has any solace, it is in history alone. The assumptions which they made and their zeal for change have a nostalgic ring to them, a ring shared by Republicans and Democrats alike. A similar attitude was held many years ago, before the State Department reluctantly concluded that what Nicaragua needed, after all, was another "strong man." But in those days, Nicaragua's strong men supported Western interests.

Today, there is neither a single dominant leader nor a single non-Marxist within the FSLN Directorate. For the time being, the Republicans in Congress, who voted strings on U.S. aid, and the present Administration, which is insisting upon such strings, are perfectly justified. The Sandinistas, on the other hand, also have a point in reminding the U.S. of the costs of another military intervention. Between the extremes of another intervention and the irrevocable Sovietization of Nicaragua, a solution is still being sought.

But at this stage in history, a solution seems remote. The FSLN has steadily and rapidly aligned Nicaragua with Cuba and the USSR. This has not been done because of U.S. hostility or any negative American reaction, alleged or real. The Carter Administration bent over backwards to provide incentives (mainly economic aid) to preserve pluralism in Nicaragua. These have failed totally to change the course of the Sandinista revolution. The Reagan Administration has made a concerted effort to build a cooperative relationship, but so far this has also failed.

It must be remembered that the FSLN did not become Marxist-Leninist overnight; it was that way from the very start. The Sandinistas do not oppose the U.S. because of what Washington does or does not do. It opposes the U.S. because of what it *is*. Like Fidel Castro in the early days of the Cuban revolution, Nicaragua's FSLN is fully committed to a Marxist-Leninist cause it has consistently espoused, in words and deeds, before and after it took power.

It is extremely doubtful that the new Administration's diplomacy—which has included a significant effort to persuade the FSLN leadership to abandon its hostility to the U.S. and support for Soviet/Cuban subversion in El Salvador—will prevent the complete consolidation of another Castro-style communist regime in Latin America. The future holds out the prospect of a major collision between the U.S. and its regional allies and Nicaragua and its Soviet/Cuban allies. Once again, the U.S. is on the horns of a persistent dilemma: one caused by the Somozas and the Sandinistas of Nicaragua.

FOOTNOTES

[1] A Communist regime was in power in Guatemala during 1954, but both the Guatemalan people and the American CIA quickly overthrew the government. For this interesting but brief episode, see L. Francis Bouchey, Alberto Piedra, *Guatemala: A Promise in Peril* (Washington, D.C.: Council for Inter-American Security, 1980), Chapter II.

[2] Harold N. Denny, *Dollars for Bullets, The Story of American Rule in Nicaragua* (N.Y.: Dial Press, 1929), p. 14.

[3] Samuel Flagg Bemis, *The Latin American Policy of the United States*, (New York: Norton, 1967), p. 106.

[4] For the best account of this story, see David McCollough, *The Path Between the Seas*, (New York: Simon and Schuster, 1977), chapters 9-14.

[5] Denny, *op. cit.*, p. 9.

[6] Edelberto Torres, in Committee on International Relations, U.S. House of Representatives, 94th Congress, 2nd sess., July 9, 1976, *Hearings Before the Subcommittee on International Organizations: Human Rights in Nicaragua, Guatemala and El Salvador* (GPO: Washington, D. C., 1976), pp. 154, 139, respectively.

[7] The middle name "Cesar" was adopted by Sandino during his war against the Marines. His original middle name was Calderon, after his mother, who was a young Indian girl. Sandino was illegitimate but maintained close ties to both parents throughout his life.

[8] This figure may be exaggerated. Eyewitnesses were said to have counted 45 bodies, but U.S. officials reported over 200 dead, and that is the figure which reached the outside press.

[9] *New York Times*, January 17, 1927, p. 4.

[10] *Ibid.*

[11] Maj. Julian C. Smith, *A Review of the Organization and Operations of the Guardia Nacional de Nicaragua* (n.p.), p. 23.

[12] *New York Times*, January 15, 1928, IX, p. 1, article by L.C. Spears.

[13] *Ibid.*, December 25, 1926, p.2.

[14] *Ibid.*, January 18, 1928, p. 3.

[15] U.S. Congress, Senate, 70th Cong., 1st sess., January 4, 1928, *Congressional Record*, Vol. 69, Part I, p. 932.

[16] Denny, *op. cit..*, p. 249.

[17] Franklin D. Roosevelt, "Our Foreign Policy," *Foreign Affairs*, July 1928, p.11.

[18] William E. Diez, *Opposition in the United States to American Policy in the Carribean, 1898-1932*, (University of Chicago, 1948), p.93.

[19] *Current Biography*, 1942, "Anastasio Somoza Garcia," p.779.

[20] John Gunther, *Inside Latin America*, (N.Y.: Harper and Brothers, 1941), p.38.

[21]The charges against Somoza were only part of the story. He personally worked around-the-clock as a symbol of leadership during the disaster crisis. While he undoubtedly profited from the relief assistance, a number of neutral investigations of his government could not find any major evidence of widespread mishandling of aid.

[22]It is still difficult to believe that Somoza had ordered Chamorro's death, especially after the numerous plots Chamorro had made against the regime in the past. In most of these he was let off easily, as a viable opposition in Nicaragua. Indeed, Chamorro was worth more to Somoza alive than dead, as events have subsequently proved.

[23]Previous quotations from "The New Nicaragua: Elections Unnecessary in 'People's Democracy,'" West Watch, Council for Inter-American Security, August-September 1981, pp. 8-9.

[24]"Moving the Miskitos," Time, March 1, 1982, p. 22. "The Indigenous People of Nicaragua's Eastern Coast: Their Treatment by the Junta of National Reconstruction," A Freedom House Report, February, 1982.

[25]"Opposition Leaders Blast 'New Dictatorship' in Nicaragua," West Watch, op. cit., p. 5.

[26]World Press Review, July 1981, p.27.

[27]"De Totalitario Califican el Proyecto de Ley de Prensa de Nicaragua," Diario Las Americas, March 13, 1982. "Press Freedom Ending in Nicaragua," The News World, March 16, 1982.

[28]Steve Frazier, "Sandinistas Tested in Nicaragua," Wall Street Journal, May 4, 1981.

[29]Nicaragua, 1980 Countries Report, U.S. Department of State, p.369.

[30]Alan Riding, "Nicaragua Ready to Talk with U.S.," New York Times, March 19, 1982, p.10.

[31]"News About Nicaragua," West Watch, op. cit., p.10.

[32]UPI, Tokyo, Japan, June 9, 1980.

[33]Quoted in Roger Reed and Juan Lulli, News Analysis: Nicaragua, Council for Inter-American Security Educational Institute, December 4, 1981, p.2.

[34]Washington Post, August 14, 1981, p.A25.

[35]Hearing, Subcommittee on Western Hemisphere Affairs, Senate Foreign Relations Committee, February 1, 1982.

[36]Hearing, Senate Foreign Relations Committee, February 2, 1981.

[37]Interview with William J. Casey, U.S. News and World Report, March 8, 1982, p.23. Morton M. Kondracke, "El Salvador, Vietnam and Central American Policy," Wall Street Journal, March 4, 1982, p.29.

[38]Patrick Tyler and Bob Woodward, "U.S. Approves Covert Plan in Nicaragua," Washington Post, March 10, 1982, p.A1.

[39]Philip Taubman, "U.S. Reportedly Sending Millions To Foster Moderates in Nicaragua," New York Times, March 11, 1982, p.1. See, also, "C.I.A.'s Nicaragua Role: A Proposal or a Reality?" New York Times, March 17, 1982.

[40]Alan Riding, "Nicaragua Asks Security Council To Rebuke U.S.," New York Times, March 20, 1982, p.1.

[41]Michael J. Berlin, "Nicaraguan Leader Blasts U.S. at U.N., Offers Negotiations," Washington Post, March 26, 1982, p.A1.

[42]"Double or Quits in Nicaragua," The Economist, March 20, 1982, p.55.

[43]Bernard Gwertzman, "Haig Is Cautious About Any Accord With Nicaraguans," New York Times, March 16, 1982, p.1.

[44]Bernard D. Nossiter, "Nicaraguan Urges U.S. To Negotiate," New York Times, March 26, 1982.

[45]Jeane Kirkpatrick, "Dictatorships and Double Standards," Commentary, November 1979, pp.37-38.

BIBLIOGRAPHY

Obviously, the published material covering nearly a century of U.S.-Nicaraguan relations is very large. I have, therefore, deliberately confined the following list to material printed only in English and only to those items which have dealt with the issues in some depth. There are hundreds of private collections and diaries, smaller pieces and thousands of newspaper and journal articles which could easily offer a bibliography of many pages. The following selection, however, is both comprehensive and representative of the important points on the historic dialogue between Washington and Managua. It will serve the interested reader well enough, and it embraces the full spectrum of fact and opinion between the Somozas and the Sandinistas.

Books

Beals, Carlton. *Banana Gold,* (Philadelphia: Lippincott, 1932).

Beaulac, Willard. *Career Ambassador,* (New York: MacMillan, 1951).

Bell, Belden. *Nicaragua: Ally Under Siege,* (Washington, D.C.: Council on American Affairs, 1977).

Cox, Isaac J. *Nicaragua and the United States,* (Boston: World Peace Foundation, 1928).

Crawley, Eduardo. *Dictators Never Die, A Portrait of Nicaragua and the Somoza Dynasty,* (New York: St. Martin's Press, 1979).

Cummins, Lejeune. *Quijote on a Burro: Sandino and the Marines,* (Mexico City: Impresora Azteca, 1958).

Denny, Harold N. *Dollars for Bullets, the Story of American Rule in Nicaragua,* (New York: Dial Press, 1929).

de Nogales, Raphael. *The Looting of Nicaragua,* (New York: Robert McBride and Co., 1928).

Diederich, Bernard. *Somoza and the Legacy of U.S. Involvement in Central America,* (New York: E.P. Dutton, 1981)

Goldwert, Marvin. *The Constabulary in the Dominican Republic and Nicaragua,* (Gainesville: University of Florida Press, 1962).

Heinl, Robert D., Jr. *Soldiers of the Sea: The United States Marine Corps, 1775-1962,* (Annapolis: U.S. Naval Institute, 1962).

Hill, Roscoe R. *Fiscal Intervention in Nicaragua,* (New York: Paul Maisel, 1933).

Kammen, William. *A Search for Stability: U.S. Diplomacy Toward Nicaragua, 1925-1933,* (University of Notre Dame Press, 1968).

MacCauley, Neill. *The Sandino Affair,* (Chicago: Quadrangle, 1967).

Millet, Richard. *Guardians of the Dynasty,* (Maryknoll, New York: Orbis Books, 1977).

Munro, Dana G. *Intervention and Dollar Diplomacy in the Caribbean, 1900-1921,* (Princeton University Press, 1964).

_____ The United States and the Caribbean Republics, 1921-1933, (Princeton University Press, 1974).

Ptacek, Kerry. *Nicaragua: A Revolution Against the Church?* (Washington, D.C.: Institute on Religion and Democracy, 1981).

Reed, Roger. *Nicaraguan Military Operations and Covert Activities in Latin America,* (Washington, D.C.: Council for Inter-American Security, 1982).

Smith, Major Julian C. *A Review of the Organization and Operations of the Guardia Nacional de Nicaragua,* (n.p.), 1937.

Somoza, Anastasio (as told to Jack Cox). *Nicaragua Betrayed,* (Boston: Western Islands, 1980).

Stimson., Henry L. *American Policy in Nicaragua,* (New York: Scribner's, 1927).

McDonald, Lawrence P. *Ally Betrayed. . . Nicaragua,* (Alexandria, Virginia: Western Goals, 1980).

Walker, Thomas. *Nicaragua: The Land of Sandino,* (Boulder, Colorado: Westview Press, 1981).

Whelan, James R. *Through the American Looking Glass: Central America's Crisis,* (Washington, D.C.: Council for Inter-American Security, 1980).

Articles

Anderson, Charles. "Nicaragua: The Somoza Dynasty," in Martin Needler (Ed.), *Political Systems of Latin America,* 2nd ed., (New York: Van Nostrand Reinhold, 1970).

Araujo, Richard. "The Nicaraguan Connection: A Threat to Central America," *Backgrounder,* The Heritage Foundation. February 24, 1982.

Bailey, Thomas A. "Interest in Nicaraguan Canal, 1903-1931," *Hispanic American Historical Review.* February 1936.

Baylen, Joseph O. "American Intervention in Nicaragua, 1909-1933," *Southwestern Social Science Quarterly.* September 1954.

Baylen, Joseph O. "Sandino: Patriot or Bandit," *Hispanic American Historical Review.* August 1951.

Beaulac, Willard. "Nicaragua," *Foreign Service Journal.* February 1980.

Beveridge, Cindy. "Sandinistas Persecute Atlantic Coast Indians," *West Watch,* Council for Inter-American Security. August-September 1981.

Buell, Raymond L. "Reconstruction in Nicaragua," *Foreign Policy Association Information Service.* November 12, 1930.

_____ "The United States and Central American Revolutions," *Foreign Policy Association Report.* July 22, 1931.

Busey, James L. "Foundations of Political Contrast, Costa Rica and Nicaragua," *Western Political Quarterly,* September 1958.

Campbell, Capt. H. Denny, "Aviation in Guerrilla Warfare," *Marine Corps Gazette.* February 1931, May 1931, and November 1931.

Carlson, Capt. Evans F. "The Guardia Nacional de Nicaragua," *Marine Corps Gazette.* August 1937.

Carter, Calvin B. "The Kentucky Feud in Nicaragua," *World's Work.* July 1927.

Christian, Shirley. "Freedom and Unfreedom in Nicaragua," *The New Republic.* July 18, 1981.

_____ "Covering the Sandinistas: The Foregone Conclusions of the Fourth Estate," *Miami Herald.* March 7, 1982.

Denig, Lt. Col. Robert L., "Native Officers Corps, Guardia Nacional de Nicaragua," *Marine Corps Gazette.* November 1932.

Dennis, Lawrence. "Nicaragua In Again, Out Again," *Foreign Affairs.* April 1931.

_____ "Revolution, Recognition, and Intervention," *Foreign Affairs.* January 1931.

Division of Operations and Training, U.S. Marine Corps. "Combat Operations in Nicaragua," *Marine Corps Gazette.* March 1929, December 1928, December 1929, September 1929, June 1929.

Dodds, Harold W. "American Supervision of the Nicaraguan Elections," *Foreign Affairs.* April 1929.

_____ "American Supervision of the Nicaraguan Election," *Marine Corps Gazette.* June 1929.

_____ "The United States and Nicaragua," *Annals of the American Academy of Political and Social Science.* July 1927.

Edson, Capt. Merritt A. "The Coco Patrol," *Marine Corps Gazette.* February 1937.

Gorman, Stephen M. "Sandinista Chess: How the Left Took Control," *Caribbean Review.* Winter 1981.

Gray, Maj. John A. "The Second Nicaraguan Campaign," *Marine Corps Gazette.* February 1933.

Hackett, Charles W. "The Death of Sandino," *Current History.* April 1934.

_____ "Relations Between the United States and Latin America Since 1898," *Current History.* September 1927.

_____ "A Review of Our Policy in Nicaragua," *Current History.* November 1928.

_____ "Sandino, Patriot or Traitor?" *Current History.* May 1934.

Kiracofe, Clifford A. "Nicaragua, Terrorism and the PLO," *West Watch,* Council for Inter-American Security. December 1980.

Kotz, Nick and Morton Kondracke. "How to Avoid Another Cuba," *The New Republic*. June 20, 1981.

LeoGrande, William M. "The Revolution in Nicaragua: Another Cuba?" *Foreign Affairs*. Fall 1979.

Ligonier, John. "Suspension of Rights Paves Way for Greater Repression in Nicaragua," *Human Events*. March 27, 1982.

McClellan, Maj. Gen. Edwin N. "The Nueva Segovia Expedition," *Marine Corps Gazette*. Part One, May 1931, and Part Two, August 1931.

McClellan, Maj. Gen. Edwin N. "The Saga of the Coco," *Marine Corps Gazette*. November 1930.

—————— "Supervising Nicaraguan Elections: 1928," *United States Naval Institute Proceedings*. January 1933.

—————— "The True Sandino," *Army and Navy Register*. March 3, 1934.

Metcalf, Lt. Col. Clyde H. "The Marine Corps and the Changing Caribbean Policy," *Marine Corps Gazette*. November 1937.

Montes, J. Antonio. "Military Buildup in Nicaragua," *West Watch*, Council for Inter-American Security. July 1981.

Montgomery, Robin Navarro. "The Fall of Somoza: Anatomy of a Revolution," *Parameters*. March 1980.

Munro, Dana G. "The Basis of Intervention in the Caribbean," *Current History*. September 1927.

—————— "The Establishment of Peace in Nicaragua," *Foreign Affairs*. July 1933.

Pearson, Neale J. "Nicaragua in Crisis," *Current History*. February 1979.

Penfield, W.S. "Emiliano Chamorro, Nicaragua's Dictator," *Current History*. June 1926.

Reed, Roger and Juan Lulli. "Nicaragua: The Consolidation of the Revolution," *New Analysis: Nicaragua,* Council for Inter-American Security Educational Institute, December 4, 1981.

Ribas, Mario. "A Central American Indictment of the United States," *Current History*. September 1927.

Rowell, Maj. Ross. "Aircraft in Bush Warfare," *Marine Corps Gazette*. September 1929.

Saenz, Vincente. "The Peaceful Penetration of Central America," *Current History*. September 1927.

Schubert, Lt. Richard H., "Communications in Bush Warfare," *Marine Corps Gazette*. June 1929.

Serafino, Nina M. "Nicaragua: U.S. Interests and Policy Options," *Issue Brief,* Library of Congress, Congressional Research Service. December 23, 1981.

Shipstead, Henrik. "Dollar Diplomacy in Latin America," *Current History*. September 1927.

Stevens, John F. "Is A Second Canal Necessary?," *Foreign Affairs*. April 1930.

St. John, Jeffery. "The Marxist Threat to Nicaragua," *Heritage Foundation Backgrounder*. July 10, 1979.

Strother, Robert S. "The New Boys in the Bunker," *National Review*. November 23, 1979.

Theberge, James D. "Rediscovering the Caribbean: U.S. Policy for the 1980's," *Commonsense*. Spring 1980.

_____"Soviet Naval Presence in the Caribbean Sea Area," in James L. George (Ed.), *Problems of Seapower as We Approach the Twenty-First Century* (Washington, D.C.: American Enterprise Institute, 1978).

Thompson, Charles A. "The Caribbean Situation: Nicaragua and El Salvador," *Foreign Policy Reports*. August 30, 1933.

Thompson, Wallace. "The Doctrine of the 'Special Interest' of the United States in the Region of the Caribbean Seas," *Annals of the Academy of Political and Social Science*. July 1927.

Thurston, Walter C. "Relations With Our Latin American Neighbors," *Annals of the American Academy of Political and Social Science*. July 1931.

Vash, Edgar. "The Turmoil of Nicaragua: From Somoza to the Sandinistas," *American Conservative Union Education and Research Institute*. September 4, 1980.

Walraven, Lt. J.C. "Typical Combat Patrols in Nicaragua," *Marine Corps Gazette*. December 1929.

Weitzel, George T. "The United States and Central America—Policy of Clay and Knox," *Annals of the Academy of Political and Social Science*. July 1927.

Williams, Brig. Gen. Dion. "Managua Disaster," *Marine Corps Gazette*. August 1931.

_____ "The Nicaraguan Situation," *Marine Corps Gazette*. November 1930.

Williams, Whiting. "Geographic Determinism in Nicaragua," *Annals of the American Academy of Political and Social Science*. July 1927.

Wright, Theodore P. "Free Elections in the Latin American Policy of the United States," *Political Science Quarterly*. March 1959.

ALLENDE:
DEATH OF A
MARXIST DREAM

A new book by James Whelan, Editor of the *Washington Times*, tells the story of the downfall of Salvador Allende, the world's first freely-elected Marxist president.

The controversy still rages. How did he die? Why did he die? Was he a martyr, an evil genius, the victim of forces he began but could not control?

Author James Whelan interviewed more than 65 persons to give this account of the generals and admirals who masterminded Allende's fall and the human drama of a violent and historical confrontation.

This 230-page, hardcover book is available for $14.95 from the Council for Inter-American Security Educational Institute, 729 Eighth Street, S.E., Suite 300, Washington, D.C. 20003.